COMPLETE GUIDE

How ... last date sta...

428

Collins

COMPLETE GUIDE

Letter Writing

How to Get Results

ESTHER SELSDON

HarperCollins*Publishers*

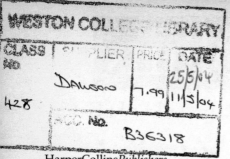
HarperCollins*Publishers*
Westerhill Road, Glasgow G64 2QT

The Collins website is www.collins.co.uk

First published 2001 as Everything You Need to Know Letter Writing
First published as Collins Letter Writing 2004

© Essential Books 2001, 2004

Reprint 10 9 8 7 6 5 4 3 2 1 0

ISBN 0 00 716558 7

A catalogue record for this book is available from the British Library

Typeset by Davidson Pre-Press Graphics Ltd, Glasgow

Printed and bound in Great Britain by Clays Ltd, St Ives plc

C O N T E N T S

INTRODUCTION   9

CHAPTER 1: Before you Begin – The Purpose   13
Why write?   14
The pen   14
Pen or mouse?   16
Choosing your materials   18
Writing tools   24

CHAPTER 2: Getting Started – The Basics   30
Is it clear?   31
How to top and tail a letter   34
Paragraphs   39
Layout   40
Titles   42

CHAPTER 3: Grammar & Punctuation   46
Why study grammar?   47
Punctuation   55
Spelling   62
Abbreviations   71
Tips on style   73

CHAPTER 4: Personal Letters   77
Presentation   78
Apologies   78
Writing to children   80
Condolences & congratulations   84
Fan mail   89
General friendship & thank you letters   90
Love letters   100
Polite requests & rude letters   109

CHAPTER 5: Business Letters   **114**
Presentation   116
Junk mail   117
Sample business letters   118

CHAPTER 6: Technical Matters   **152**
Headings   153
Presenting facts   153
Memos   155

CHAPTER 7: Employment Correspondence   **156**
Job applications   157
References   159
Rejections   162
Letters of resignation   162
Complimenting an employee   163
Reprimands   164
Dismissals   166

CHAPTER 8: Communicating with the Media   **169**
Requesting media coverage   169
Declining media coverage   172
Letters to the editor   173
Personal letter   174
Specific articles   175
General grievance letter   176

CHAPTER 9: Legal Matters   **179**
Libel   180
Your rights   182
Copyright   183
Without prejudice   185
Communication with solicitors   186
Threatening legal action   188

CHAPTER 10: The Electronic Age   **191**
Email   192
World wide web   208
Faxes   213

CHAPTER 11: Filing Correspondence   **216**
Filing   217
Keeping copies   219
Security & Data Protection Act, 1984   220
Creating an archive   221

CHAPTER 12: Postage   **222**
Envelopes   223
Types of postage   227
Poste restante   230
Forwarding mail   231
Small packets   231
Private mail systems   232
Appendices   235

INTRODUCTION

Despite the invention of the telephone and the apparent casualness of many of our 21st-century arrangements, the written word is still the politest, most permanent means of communication and still the only really satisfactory way to deal with legal and professional correspondence. This makes letter-writing sound horribly responsible and, to many people, putting even the simplest of thoughts on paper to good effect does seem like a daunting task. But it needn't be. There are basic rules of good grammar, style and approach that can be broken down into their component parts for anyone to learn and follow. This book lists those rules and helps to break down those parts and, in the process, makes the acquisition of good letter-writing skills a more entertaining exercise.

But this is the 21st century and we are now in the modern age of communication. Explanatory chapters on joining the email and internet age are included because it is a rapidly changing world out there and you never know when you might need to employ some of these constantly evolving e-trends. In the same vein, other chapters include sample pro-forma letters that deal with those everyday situations for which you might need to write a precise, businesslike letter but don't quite know where to start. Of course, the reader can, and should, customise and adapt these model letters to suit their own style and their own needs but a helping hand might just save time.

We all need to write. Whether this be to a lawyer, to a friend or even to someone we don't happen to like that much, a well-expressed letter may make a small but crucial difference. Stronger, more powerful correspondence can eliminate further unnecessary business correspondence or, even more impressively, might make social correspondence a more regular, more entertaining affair. It's worth a go. Give it a try.

WHAT THE ICONS MEAN

The Web Tip icon alerts you to where relevant website addresses appear in the text. If you are browsing through the book or specifically looking for website information, these icons will take you straight there.

WEB TIP

Helpful tips throughout have been highlighted in tinted panels.

> ☞ Write a letter by hand rather than using a word processor if you want it to be more personal or intimate.

1

BEFORE YOU BEGIN

THE PURPOSE

- WHY WRITE?
- THE PEN
- PEN OR MOUSE?
- CHOOSING YOUR MATERIALS
- WRITING TOOLS

WITWOUD: Madam, do you pin up
Your hair with all your letters?
MILLAMANT: Only with those in verse, Mr
Witwoud. I never pin up my hair with prose.

William Congreve, *The Way of the World* (1700)

Why not telephone? Before you set pen to paper or mouse to mat, ask yourself why you need to write a letter. Think about your reason for writing. Do you want, or need, to make a permanent statement and, if you do, and your letter is put in a box and filed, would you be embarrassed to see that very same letter turn up again in twenty-five years' time? These are the first questions to ask yourself when you think about whether you should be writing a letter at all.

Generally speaking, we write because the process of putting words to paper is more effective than speech. It demands the sole attention of the recipient while being read and can be more intimate than speech; it is certainly more durable.

WHY WRITE?

Hundreds of letters are opened every morning. You will want your particular missive to be the one that is clearest on the page and therefore read first, and you will want it to be understood immediately and acted upon without delay.

Ask yourself:

- Do I know what my message is?

- If yes, then is my message necessary?

- If yes, then is the recipient my friend?

- If yes, then would a telephone call be more appropriate?

- If no, then is this mainly a social or a professional communication?

- If professional, then am I trying to make an impression?

- If yes, then will I be embarrassed to be reminded that this letter exists in a year's time?

- If no, then continue.

THE PEN

The modern fountain pen was invented by Lewis Edson Waterman in 1883 and technology hasn't looked back since. Waterman created a special device which managed to slow down the ink feed to the nib and thereby reduced the chances of any extra ink leaking from the pen. The age-old habit, familiar to cinema-goers all over the world, of dipping a quill into an ink pot was instantly eliminated. Writing became faster – and faster still in 1943 when Laszlo Biro, a Hungarian inventor, patented his quick-drying, ball-point pen. Since Biro's new invention did not leak at high altitude and could even be used underwater, it was offered as a writing tool to US and UK forces during the Second World War. It was an immediate hit. But the revolution had only just begun.

The world's first 'proper' computer was built in 1948. It was called the Manchester Mark I and stored and processed any information fed into it very quickly by use of an electronic transistor.

In 1958 Texas Instruments, an American firm, produced the first integrated circuit or silicon chip. All the electrical components in the computer were now combined into one slice of silicon, a type of quartz which was grown artificially and cut into very thin slices. Up to 500 chips could be made from each of these slices and each of these chips could contain, in turn, up to 500 photographic copies of the design of the electrical circuit. In layman's terms, silicon chips are minute and contain a lot of information. The silicon chip enabled the arrival, in 1982, of the word-processor as a mainstream writing tool. Nowadays, things are even easier. Computer programmes have been developed which introduce the concept of formula letters, facilitate the addressing of envelopes and introduce the idea of instant mass mailing.

> ☞ Write a letter by hand rather than using a word processor if you want it to be more personal or intimate.

We now have a whole spectrum of ways to convey our message. The crucial part is deciding which is the right one for you. Just because a word-processing programme exists, this doesn't mean that you necessarily have to use it. The decision is yours.

Main types of communication:

- handwriting
- word-processed letter
- fax
- email

Ask yourself:

- Is this letter to a friend?

- Is it urgent?

- Is it complicated?

- Is it personal?

- Does it involve figures and charts?

- Should you have written it yesterday?

- In what form would you want to receive this information?

PEN OR MOUSE?

Of any courteous letters, now: There are so few.

Ben Jonson (1616)

Once you have come to grips with the idea that your letter may exist for ever, and yet have still decided to take the plunge, then your next step must be to decide on the most suitable medium for your communication. Is the correspondence friendly, is it an apology and how much information needs to be imparted?

Writing is a slow business. We think much more quickly than we write and pen and ink merely add to the laboriousness of the process. If you wish to convey the idea that you have poured precious, loving care into your correspondence, then old-fashioned penmanship would be the most suitable choice.

Handwritten letters, in other words, demonstrate the fact that the person who sent them *cares*.

☞ A printed letter can be impersonal but will always be legible.

The main negative aspect of a handwritten letter, mundane though it might be, is that a lot of people's handwriting is not very pretty. There's really little point putting in the extra time if no one will be able to read your letter anyway. Be honest with yourself. Is your handwriting easily legible? You already know what you are trying to say. Bear in mind that your reader might have to guess.

Word-processing is the composition of a document using a personal computer. Clearly, when a lot of facts are involved a word-processed letter will always be more effective, but for, say, a bereavement note it might be totally inappropriate. The process of computing can sometimes make the task of letter writing seem very industrial and rather formal but the results are sure to look modern, clear and businesslike.

On the plus side, with today's printers, you can choose a particular font or paper size or graphic design in order to make your word-processed letter look softer or more casual. In any event, the printed letter is now so ubiquitous that a typewritten letter is unlikely to send out any particular signals. There are, today, very few occasions when even a social correspondent would be shocked to receive a letter in a printed format – although, of course, it is still more flattering to receive a handwritten communication.

Handwritten	Word-processed
Wedding congratulations	Letter to bank
Bereavement	CV
Love letters	Letters featuring
Birth congratulations	graphs or facts
	Explanatory letters

There is one pitfall to this apparent ease of communication, however, which many computer users fail to see. Just because it looks good instantaneously, doesn't mean it's necessarily right. The words flow fast – communication speeds are beginning to catch up with the speed of thought – but that doesn't make them lovely. It is very easy to miss a mistake on a screen and it is very easy to believe that your letter is as stylish in content as it is in appearance. Just remember that it may not be …

Word-processed letters, in other words, demonstrate the fact that the person who sent them is a *professional*.

CHOOSING YOUR MATERIALS

Once again, think about the kind of impression you are trying to convey. Do you wish to be seen as a formal or a casual correspondent, and should the tone of your letter be friendly, brusque or merely factual? Once you have decided whether your letter is personal, business or other correspondence, you can choose which material is best suited to convey your desired tone.

Ask yourself:

- what are you trying to achieve by writing?

- do you like the recipient?

- is that a relevant question?

If the answer to the last question is 'no', then you should definitely be word-processing.

PAPER

HEADED OR UNHEADED? The letters that you send are an expression of your personality. They signify to the world outside how you would like to be seen and they do this before you have even reached the end of your first sentence. The wrong stationery may, therefore, create entirely the wrong impression before the contents of your letter have even been considered. Given this factor, it's probably a good idea to make the correct stationery selection at the very beginning of the process. You're just giving yourself all the advantages you can.

ILLUSTRATION 1   *Headed paper can be kept simple and needn't be expensive*

Historically, it was considered correct to have headed paper for business correspondence and plain paper for personal. Things have moved on. Nowadays it is imperative to have headed paper for business letters and unusual not to have it for personal correspondence. Headed paper makes life easier for the recipient. If he or she feels the urge to reply straight away then he or she won't have to go digging around in old files and address books in order to get the required information. The necessary information, by the way, includes an accurate postcode as well as a telephone number (with full area code) and, if possible, an email address. It is not really necessary, and possibly inelegant, to include your name, as this will be at the bottom of your letter in any event.

☞ **The right kind of stationery, especially headed paper, can make all the difference.**

It may also be considered slightly suspect to write a personal letter on unheaded paper. If you have the recipient's correct address and you must do, since you are writing to them, then why shouldn't they have all your particulars? Mutuality breeds trust.

Unheaded paper may be suitable for friends whom you know well. It may also be suitable for covering letters accompanying other materials or for very brief notes to almost anyone, but, generally speaking, when in doubt, and if at all possible, stick to headed. It looks more attractive.

Headed paper, though, doesn't necessarily have to be fancy embossed stationery ordered from an upmarket stationery firm. For simple business correspondence, and certainly for friends, it is perfectly acceptable simply to print your headed paper at home on your own printer. However, professionally printed paper, unless you have all the latest technology, is normally smarter. In this particular case, it seems, you pay for what you get. Appearance may not make any difference to the end result of your correspondence, but, on the other hand, it may. Again, it's best to use all the advantages you can.

Keep the design simple and the print bold and make sure that the words are large enough to read easily.

PAPER TYPES

Use the best-quality paper that you feel you can afford. Bond paper is paper that will not tear or crease easily. It is specially designed for letter writing and is recommended for all business, and social, communications. As a general rule, thick paper is good paper and 100g is an adequate weight to choose.

> ☞ Try not to use flimsy paper unless you are writing a letter to be posted to or from abroad.

Bank paper is a thin paper that is generally used for file copies. It is not recommended for the actual letter that you intend to post. You should try to avoid using any flimsy or particularly thin paper: it's quite difficult to handle and it looks a bit cheapskate. The recipient may be worried that it might tear. It is also, quite often, difficult to thread bank-type paper successfully through a printer since the pages may cause the machine to jam as they go through.

If you are abroad, however, and writing to friends at home, then it would make sense to use thin paper, or even airmail paper, since this will cost less to post.

If you care about the environment, you may wish to use recycled stationery. This might be considered slightly startling in some business circles but certainly shouldn't be. Recycled stationery is becoming more and more common and is easily purchased in most decent stationery shops.

PAPER SIZES

Paper these days comes in a variety of standardised sizes – all of which are referred to as 'A' sizes. From both the manufacturer's and the customer's point of view, this is handy, since everyone knows what everyone else is talking about, and it is easy to calculate since each A size is exactly half the area of the previous one, in a descending scale from A0 to A7. An A2 sheet folded in half will, therefore, produce two A3 sheets. One A3 sheet will produce two A4 sheets and so on.

The most frequently used sizes, these days, are A3, A4 and A5, and most professional correspondence will be on A4 paper since filing systems are organised specifically around this size. Most shop-purchased single-sheet writing paper comes in standard A4 size, largely because of this factor.

A3 It would be very unusual to write a letter on A3 paper. It would be almost impossible to fold out and read, let alone stuff into an envelope. It is more generally suitable for writing with accompanying drawings, page layouts and large spreadsheets.

A4 This is the standard size for letters. You can expect any regular business letter that you might send or receive to be printed on A4 paper. It creates a businesslike, clean look and is extremely handy to print out since it will fit perfectly into your printer hopper without having to make possibly complex adjustments. It is what people expect both for themselves and for their filing systems. Business correspondence should be typed on one side only, using continuation sheets for the second and subsequent pages.

A5 This notelet size tends to arise more frequently in card than in flexible paper format. It might be suitable for a very brief note or if your business letter is very short and will cause a sheet of A4 paper to appear slightly bald. If this might be the case, consider investing in some A5 paper which has a distinctive, old-fashioned appearance and may be more appropriate.

COLOUR

It is simply a matter of common sense that you should use a colour of paper which is appropriate for the occasion. Canary yellow is unlikely to be correct for a letter of bereavement while pink for a CV might be jolly but is unlikely to get you the job. A single colour is almost always preferable and certainly more elegant than sheets of paper covered with spots and stars. White paper will merely define you as 'standard' and this could be a good thing. Cream is slightly more sophisticated but, possibly, too delicate for a bold business letter demanding attention. Cream suggests an extra layer of refinement and sophistication. Is this the impression you are trying to convey?

Other colours range from the bold to the bizarre. If you are writing to a designer, for example, then you may wish to appear design-led, but

---

☞ **Never use lined paper – it looks as if you are still learning the alphabet.**

pause to think about whether this image might be more effectively displayed with a small but potent logo in the bottom corner of the page, for example. Try to achieve the perfect balance between creativity with flair and coming across as pretentious or simply too loud and attention-seeking.

Marbled paper, particularly the hand-painted varieties from certain Tuscan villages, can be stunning, but bear in mind that they may not make the clearest backgrounds for print. Always check you can read the text before plumping for this option. Embossed and edged papers are very fancy and probably inappropriate unless you're inviting guests to a very grand event like a wedding. In any other circumstances, using such decorative flourishes might simply be seen as flashy.

POSTCARDS

Apart from when they are on holiday, many people no longer use postcards as a method of communication, although they are, on certain occasions, the perfect medium on which to write a letter. Though this probably isn't a huge factor, they may save you money on an envelope, and writing on both sides of a blank postcard can create space for quite a long message, even though it might be one that still feels very casual.

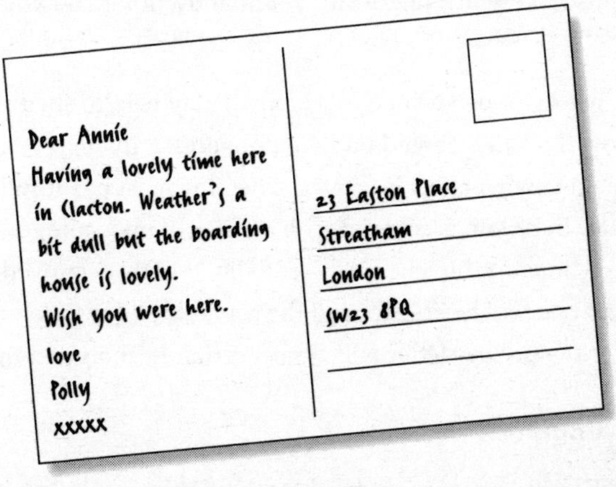

Dear Annie
Having a lovely time here
in Clacton. Weather's a
bit dull but the boarding
house is lovely.
Wish you were here.
love
Polly
xxxxx

23 Easton Place
Streatham
London
SW23 8PQ

ILLUSTRATION 2   Typical postcard layout. Keep your message brief

For any brief message, a postcard is ideal, although clearly not when this message contains confidential or personal information. They are particularly suitable when sending 'thank-you' notes for gifts or for a dinner invitation, since you don't need to say the same thing several different ways just to fill the page.

When choosing a postcard, think about both the message you want to convey and the personality of the recipient. A comic illustration may be good for your college friend but singularly inappropriate for your aunt or one of your work colleagues. Plain postcards, these days, tend to be enclosed inside envelopes anyway, so, if you are considering one of these, you might just as well use A5 headed cards. Postcards with subdued works of art tend to be suitable for just about anybody. If you want to appear sophisticated, always choose this more general variety rather than the type that displays a saucy image of a seaside pier.

WRITING TOOLS

There is a very wide range of writing tools from which to choose. Ball-point, fountain pen or felt tip are all possible. You need to make a decision about which might be the appropriate one for your particular requirements (and which might suit your handwriting and your message).

The short history of pen technology (above) may help to shed some light on how they all emerged but will not necessarily help you to choose. Imagine what effect is created when the most beautifully written letter in Britain is covered with a series of ink smudges and strange, psychopathic blotches. All credibility will be destroyed. On top of which, no one will be able to read the contents and people will not take you seriously. Your letter will almost certainly end up in the bin.

FOUNTAIN PEN

Many traditionalists, and many aesthetes, still think of the fountain pen as the classic means with which to write a handwritten letter. It looks amazingly elegant; you can choose the colour of your ink and it allows for the full potential sensuality of writing. The most effective love letters tend to be written in fountain pen.

> ☞ Do not attempt to use a fountain pen if you don't think your handwriting is up to it.

Most people use black or blue ink but any coloured ink will do. Pale blue is not too wacky but makes a personal statement and tends to look slightly more feminine than dark blue. Many literary men have preferred to use brown ink since it is, similarly, slightly more personal in appearance but not too brazen. Bear in mind, if choosing a pale colour, that it must still be legible on the page and that yellows tend to fade from view even before arriving at the recipient's door. Also bear in mind that fountain pens can scratch the paper if you are not careful, and this is clearly not a good thing.

BIRO

Biros are a step down from fountain pens in sophistication but they have their own advantages. For one thing, they do not, generally, smudge. They may not require quite the concentration or hand control that fountain pens do and they are not as wet. A biro is certainly an appropriate tool with which to write a postcard or a casual memo or note to a colleague. It is also, of course, much easier to transport than a fountain pen, since it will not automatically require extra paraphernalia like cartridges and bottles and, on a practical note, is relatively unlikely to leak into your coat pocket.

> ☞ A fountain pen may give your writing more character than a biro, but a biro is far more convenient and practical.

Most biros tend to be filled with black or blue ink. Similar rules about colour apply as for the pen. Other colours might be fine if your recipient works in the world of art or fashion. Otherwise, they might find bright orange both illegible and a bit eccentric.

FELT TIP

Felt tip is really best saved for the clear marking of envelopes. Most felt-tip nibs are quite broad and difficult to wield and they tend to remind people of their primary school. But they are excellent for writing on difficult surfaces, like a Jiffy bag.

TYPEFACES

Typeface is the word for the style of print that you are using on the page. There are many different kinds of typeface and each might appeal to a different kind of customer. Generally speaking, the two most common typefaces for business communication are Arial and Times New Roman. Arial is a bold, round sort of typeface without excessive adornment. Times New Roman tends to look slightly more serious since it is thinner and longer and the letters have all their formal curlicues, base lines and the *n*, for example, has its back hook at the top of the first stroke. This cross-line finishing off the stroke of a letter is called a serif. Characters without cross-lines (as in an Arial typeface) are referred to as 'sans-serif', from the French, meaning 'without a serif'.

EXERCISE

1 Compare these typefaces.

2 Decide which one you like the best and consider why.

3 Consider which you find easiest to read.

4 Compare each text extract, which is the opening paragraph of a novel by Dickens, with its designated typeface and decide whether the two could be said to match in style.

5 Think briefly about your friends and decide which typeface
   you might use to write to each of them.

HELVETICA

My father's family name being Pirrip, and my Christian name
Philip, my infant tongue could make of both names nothing longer
or more explicit than Pip. So I called myself Pip, and came to be
called Pip.

Charles Dickens, 'Great Expectations' (1860)

This is a piece of prose supposedly describing someone's
childhood nickname. The written style is simple and the typeface
is sans-serif and quite childlike in appearance. There is quite an
appropriate match between style and content.

IMPACT

It was the best of times, it was the worst of times, it was the age of
wisdom, it was the age of foolishness, it was the epoch of belief, it was
the epoch of incredulity, it was the season of Light, it was the season of
Darkness, it was the spring of hope, it was the winter of despair.

Charles Dickens, A Tale of Two Cities (1859)

This is quite an epic opening to a novel. It is a declaration of
a whole state of being and written in a distinctly Victorian style.
The typeface looks quite modern, which is at odds with the period
style of the writing, and lacks authority. The typeface is therefore
at variance with the text both in feel and in appearance.

BRITANNIC BOLD

In these times of ours, though concerning the exact year there is no need to be precise, a boat of dirty and disreputable appearance, with two figures in it, floated on the Thames, between Southwark Bridge which is of iron, and London Bridge which is of stone, as an autumn evening closing in.

Charles Dickens, 'Our Mutual Friend' (1865)

This is a perfectly straightforward piece of descriptive prose with a touch of mystery to it. The typeface has certain old-fashioned characteristics – most notably on the 'g' – and, although it captures a little of the air of mystery about the piece, it's not really clear enough to sustain a narrative of any length.

GOUDY TEXT

In the year 1775, there stood upon the borders of Epping Forest, at a distance of about twelve Miles from London – measuring from the Standard in Cornhill, or rather from the spot on or near to which the Standard used to be in days of yore – a house of public entertainment called the Maypole; which fact was demonstrated to all such travellers as could neither read nor write (and at that time a vast number both of travellers and stay-at-homes were in this condition) by the emblem reared on the roadside over against the house.

Charles Dickens, 'Barnaby Rudge' (1841)

This is an opening which immediately conjures up a picture of 'days of yore'. Apart from the fact that the typeface is quite difficult to read, its high decorative values make it look quite antique. It is not a bad match, but not a perfect one either.

DOLMEN

As no lady or gentleman, with any claims to polite breeding, can possibly sympathise with the Chuzzlewit Family without being first assured of the extreme antiquity of the race, it is a great satisfaction to know that it undoubtedly descended in a direct line from Adam and Eve; and was, in the very earliest times, closely connected with the agricultural interest.

Charles Dickens, 'Martin Chuzzlewit' (1843)

The sentence is, again, quite a portentous one but in a rather more modest way. The author is clearly suggesting that the Chuzzlewits consider themselves to be a very distinguished family and he is slightly ridiculing them for this. The typeface is, for one thing, rather difficult to read. There is nothing in the text to suggest that this is an appropriate typeface.

There are no right answers: it is a question of personal taste, tact and common sense.

IS A LETTER NECESSARY?

Once again, and before you finally start writing, spend another few moments considering whether your letter really needs to be written at all. If it is a thank-you note or an apology, would it be more appropriate to telephone and speak to the recipient in person? Is it an issue that has already been aired at such length in conversation that a letter would merely add insult to injury? If the letter involves a highly confidential or delicate business matter, is the idea of committing your message to paper really the best way to proceed? If the facts might imminently result in a law suit, would it be better to consult a solicitor before putting pen to paper? Think about tact, tone and confidentiality. This may seem like repetitive advice but, in the long run, it could save you a lot of time and trouble.

2

GETTING STARTED
THE BASICS

- IS IT CLEAR?
- HOW TO TOP AND TAIL
- PARAGRAPHS
- LAYOUT
- TITLES

This is the manner in which you, as an individual, express your thoughts. There is quite a lot of confusion about the definition and meaning of writing style. Don't get too weighed down by all this but simply try to bear in mind that if you really know what you want to say then your style should select itself.

Extensive reading of good literature will always improve your own writing skills, even if this merely helps to increase your vocabulary, but, however much you read, the first rule of good style is always the same: be clear, simple and straightforward. If you are clear about your message, everything else will follow.

- Always decide what you want to say before you start writing.

- Ask yourself what your letter is about.

- At the end of every paragraph, ask yourself what you are trying to say.

- Always read your letter out loud so that you hear how it might sound to the recipient.

- Check whether it sounds natural.

- Decide whether it conveys your meaning.

IS IT CLEAR?

EXERCISE

Read the following letter and then decide:

1 Which adjectives you would use to describe the writer's style.

2 What impression of himself the writer thinks he is creating.

3 What impression of himself he is really creating.

To Madame de Meurteuil

I shall not be seeing you today, my love, and here are my reasons, which I beg you will indulgently accept.

Yesterday, instead of returning here directly, I stopped at the Countess of ____'s, which was not far out of my way, and stayed there for dinner. I did not arrive in Paris until nearly seven o'clock, when I made my way to the Opera where I hoped you might be.

After the performance, I went to revisit my acquaintance of the green-room. There I found my old friend Emilie surrounded by a host of admirers of both sexes for whom she was that very evening to provide supper at P_, I had no sooner joined the company when the invitation was, by general acclaim, extended to me, and in particular by a short and corpulent little man, who jabbered it out in Dutchman's French. He I perceived to be the real hero of the occasion, I accepted.

On the way I learned that the house we were bound for represented the price fixed upon for Emilie's favours to this grotesque creature and that the evening's supper was in fact to be a sort of wedding feast. The little man could not contain his delight at the prospect of the happiness he was soon to enjoy. He looked so pleased with himself that I was tempted to disturb his complacency: which, as it happens, is what I did.

My only difficulty lay in prevailing upon Emilie: the burgomaster's riches had made her a little scrupulous. After some hesitation, however, she gave her approval to my plan for glutting the little beer-barrel with wine, so putting him hors de combat for the rest of the night.

The high opinion we had formed of Dutch drinkers led us to employ every known method in our attempts: which succeeded so well that at dessert he no longer had strength enough to hold up his glass. Nevertheless the obliging Emilie and I continud to vie with each other in filling it up. He collapsed at length under the table in a drunken stupor such as cannot but last for a week. We decided then to send him back to Paris, and as he had not kept his carriage, I had him packed into mine and remained behind in his place. Whereupon I received the compliments of the company who retired soon after leaving me in possession of the field. So much amusement, and perhaps my long retirement, has made me find Emilie so desirable that I have promised to stay with her until the Dutchman returns to life.

This kindness I confer in exchange for one she has just done me. I have been using her for a desk upon which to write to my fair devotee – to whom I find it amusing I should send a letter written in bed, in the arms, almost, of a trollop, in which I give her an exact account of my situation and my conduct. Emilie, who read it, split her sides laughing: I hope you will laugh too.

As my letter must be franked in Paris, I am sending it to you; I leave it open. Be so good as to read it, to seal it....Good-bye, my love.

P___

Letter 47 in *Les Liaisons Dangereuses (Dangerous Liaisons)*, by Choderlos de Laclos, from the Vicomte de Valmont to Madame de Meurteuil.

ANSWERS

1 A possible list of answers might include: sarcastic, cynical and bitter.

2 As above, plus his great wit, his good taste, his sophistication and, above all, his cleverness.

3 He is manipulative, intelligent and vain. He cares little for other people and yet is tremendously anxious about what image he strikes with them. He is selfish, cynical and thoroughly unpleasant.

This is one of the most famous fictional letters in French literature precisely because Choderlos de Laclos has managed to create a really interesting, witty and clever villain without making him in any way likeable. One of the characteristics that makes the character so menacing is that his style is so perfectly formed but, like that of Wilde's Dorian Gray, contains a seething mass of corruption underneath. Style isn't all. Just because the Vicomte de Valmont is, undoubtedly, clever and entertaining, that doesn't make him nice.

> ☞ Simple is best. Say what you mean. Only say it once.

The lessons one might learn from this exercise are to avoid using superfluous words and to steer carefully away from ludicrously inappropriate adjectives. It is sensible to avoid repetition wherever you can. If the reader needs to clarify your message, they may simply get the letter back out and reread it.

If you have to use adjectives, try not to use the same ones over and over again – 'It's lovely weather here in Bournemouth and our hotel is really lovely. We are having a lovely time.' This is both boring and irritating to read. If you wish to emphasise a particular point it may well be necessary to repeat information but do try to vary the format, the sentence structure, or merely the order in which the words fall in the sentence. All these will make your letter more interesting to read and therefore more likely to be acted upon.

HOW TO TOP AND TAIL A LETTER

BEGINNING: Starting a letter badly can ruin the impression you are trying to create even before you begin writing. It goes without saying that most English correspondence begins with the word 'Dear'. Letters have used this format since the 17th century and there is no real alternative to the formula in the English language.

This may sound obvious, but it is absolutely crucial to get the recipient's name correct. If you do not bother to find out the exact spelling of their name, including their initials, titles and hyphens, you cannot really expect them to be well disposed towards you. People care about their names and to get them wrong generally indicates that you have not really put enough effort into your communication. If you don't take those extra few minutes to get these things right, then why should the recipient make an effort? It is not difficult to check. Simply telephone the person's office and ask the switchboard or the secretary for the correct spelling of the name in question. Nobody will find this in any way peculiar.

When writing to a woman, try to address her correctly and exactly as she would wish to be addressed. Check first whether she is 'Miss', 'Mrs' or 'Ms', 'Dr' or anything else. It is really annoying to be given the incorrect title. Writing to a man is not quite as hazardous but the same rules apply.

'Dear Sir' is very formal and should really be used only for particularly impersonal correspondence, including letters to public organisations or law firms. It should not really be used when addressing specific individuals within those firms. If you want a positive response from one of these anonymous and immense organisations, however, it would always be sensible to ring them up first and ask for the name of an individual within the department with which you are trying to do business. If you do not name a specific recipient, your letter may go to the bottom of a slush pile of post and may then take weeks to be read. Again, telephone the switchboard and ask for the correct name and title of a suitable individual.

Modifications of the word 'Dear' should be used with caution. '*My dear X*' can sound patronising and old-fashioned. Launching into a letter without using the word 'dear' at all – '*Lily, how are you?*', for example – could be taken as implying that Lily is not dear, and, in fact, that you probably don't like her. It might be staid and conventional, but to avoid the potential negativity of this impression it's best to stick to the safety of 'Dear'.

ENDING: If you have begun your letter with the recipient's own name (whether this be surname or first name), then you should always end your letter with the phrase 'Yours sincerely'. Yours begins with a capital *Y* while the *s* of sincerely is in lower case.

> ☞ **Start with 'Dear Tom,' end with 'Yours sincerely'.**

If you have begun your letter with the phrase 'Dear Sir' or 'Dear Madam', then you should end with the phrase 'Yours faithfully'.

> ☞ **Start with 'Dear Sir' (or Madam), end with 'Yours faithfully'.**

And that is basically the rule.

All other phrases are merely modifications of this formula. If you particularly like someone, or don't want to appear too formal, then signing off with the word 'Yours' is a good middle option. 'Best wishes' might suffice if you are writing to a relative with whom you are not particularly friendly or to a close colleague with whom you feel you have a really good working relationship.

Name & full address of recipient

Clear address, complete postcode

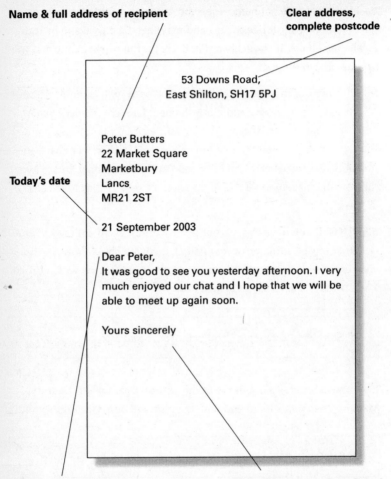

53 Downs Road,
East Shilton, SH17 5PJ

Peter Butters
22 Market Square
Marketbury
Lancs
MR21 2ST

Today's date

21 September 2003

Dear Peter,
It was good to see you yesterday afternoon. I very much enjoyed our chat and I hope that we will be able to meet up again soon.

Yours sincerely

'Dear' plus appropriate title

'Yours sincerely' as 'Dear Peter' was used at the beginning, not 'Dear Sir'

ILLUSTRATION 3   Basic layout for a standard letter

'Love' should, not unreasonably, be reserved for personal correspondence and, even then, only for people for whom it might be appropriate. Your parents, your children and your siblings are obvious contenders. If you're a woman, you can use 'love' for all your close friends also. If you're a man, you might not want to.

The very final element of your letter will be your signature. Your signature represents you. Most people, when composing formal correspondence, sign themselves with an initial for their first name and then conclude with their full surname: 'J. Author'. More fulsome souls might sign themselves 'Jemima Author', which is fine but suggests that you want the recipient to know your first name. Anything longer than this, however, merely takes up a lot of paper and looks rather self-seeking. Anything shorter – 'Jemima' – is certainly inappropriate for business correspondence. Bear in mind that your signature might not be absolutely legible, so always try to print your full name underneath your signature so that the recipient knows exactly how to spell it, should he or she need to reply.

ADDRESSES

You should always include your own address, preferably across the top of the page. If you have headed notepaper, the matter is settled for you, but if you don't, then it is very rude not to supply your own details.

✔ **DO include the recipient's name and address at the top left of the page in full.**

Always use the recipient's full postcode – what's the point of getting this wrong, even on quite a short letter? If you don't know the correct code then you can telephone the recipient's office and check. It takes a few seconds and will ensure that your letter gets there as quickly as possible. If you don't want to ring the office, you can ring the Royal Mail Postcode Enquiries desk who will tell you the exact postcode for the address you have written down. You can also check postcodes on the web at

WEB TIP
http://afis.postoffice.co.uk:8080/RoyalMail/PBS/pcodefin.asp.

It is correct to follow the number of the building by a comma, but common practice these days is to leave it out.

✔ **DON'T place the name of any house in inverted commas. It looks really messy and slightly old-fashioned.**

In professional correspondence there should be no comma at the end of each line of the address. In personal correspondence, a comma may be used at the end of each line if you feel the recipient might appreciate a truly old-fashioned style. Use your discretion.

Always remember to use the recipient's postcode, even on quite a short letter.

MAIN COUNTY ABBREVIATIONS

Berkshire	Berks
Buckinghamshire	Bucks
Cambridgeshire	Cambs
Hampshire	Hants
Lancashire	Lancs
Middlesex	Middx
Northamptonshire	Northants
Nottinghamshire	Notts
Oxfordshire	Oxon
Warwickshire	Warks
Wiltshire	Wilts
Yorkshire	Yorks

(See appendix on p. 236 for a full list of conventional county abbreviations.)

DATES

Every letter should be dated.

Standard business practice is to leave a double-spaced gap after the recipient's full address and then put the date directly below the address on the left-hand side of the page.

There are many correct ways to date a letter but the most common in business practice is to put the date in figures and then to write the month in letters with no extra punctuation. In other words, like this:

14 February 2003

Using figures only, i.e. 14/02/03, is perfectly valid but tends to look as if the letter has come straight out of a computer print-out and is rather inelegant. Adding 'st', 'th' or other such abbreviations after the number does not look very professional.

> ☞ Adding 'st','th' or other abbreviations after a date –
> '1st' or '4th' – never looks professional.

Personal correspondence is much more flexible. Using the same example, many people would write:

14th February, 2003

Note the addition of the 'th' after 14 and the comma after February, both of which make the date appear a bit more personalised and also traditional. Even in personal correspondence, however, it is probably a good idea to add the year.

PARAGRAPHS

A paragraph is composed of several sentences dealing with the same subject. In business terms, of course, much of your letter is going to be dealing with the same subject and one paragraph for a two-page document would be extremely difficult to read. Where you break your paragraphs should, therefore, be a matter of common sense.

> ☞ The aim of letter writing is to convey information.

Generally speaking, a paragraph should not be more than about fifteen or twenty lines and, in most cases, much shorter than that. There are no fixed rules, but bear in mind that the point of a paragraph is clarity of expression and that short paragraphs are infinitely preferable to long ones.

Business letters tend to be 'aligned left' which means that all paragraphs start on the left-hand side of the page and none are indented. This gives a clean, neat look and appears businesslike. When preparing semi-professional letters – to a school head teacher, for example – it may be appropriate to indent the first line of each paragraph since this is a throwback to handwritten letter style and might seem more elegant.

Handwritten letters almost always indent at the beginning of each paragraph on the basis that anything that makes handwriting easier to read is a good thing.

The rest of the layout will depend on the length of your letter. Most of us have received letters which begin at the top corner of the page and then fill the entire blank space with no margins and hardly any paragraphs. This is not going to facilitate the reading of your letter.

LAYOUT

The purpose of good layout is to make your letter clear to read and, if possible, attractive to look at. It will look most presentable if it is well spaced on the page, with approximately 2cm of margin space all around the letter, although the bottom margin should be slightly wider than that at the top of the page. If the letter is short on text, try using double-spaced lines. This avoids the page looking bald. On the other hand, if the letter is very long, it may run down to the bottom of the page, leaving you barely enough room for your signature. This also looks unprofessional. Try to avoid this by leaving less space between the address and the date, or by leaving more space at the foot of the page and then running a whole paragraph on to another page. Having just a few lines on a continuation sheet is clearly daft.

FOOTNOTES AND POSTSCRIPTS

Before you sign your letter, do make sure that it includes everything you have in mind. A PS can always be added as an afterthought, although, with word-processing today, it should hardly be necessary. If you do add a PS (or 'postscript', which derives from the Latin for 'after the writing'), bear in mind that it might well be the most instantly eye-catching item on the page, so make sure that what you say in it is of note. If you have thought carefully about your letter beforehand, you should not really need to use the PS.

> ☞ Use a PS only where really necessary.

Footnotes, on the other hand, are really designed for use in academic or technical writing. They may help to shed extra light on some part of the text which, if explained within the text itself, would destroy the natural flow of the basic argument. They are most often used to explain the sources of quotations or factual information – explanations which would not fit within the text itself.

EXAMPLE

Having visited many more rooms than could be supposed to be of any other use than to contribute to the window tax,[1] and find employment for the housemaids, 'Now,' said Mrs Rushworth, 'we are coming to the chapel, which properly we ought to enter from above, and look down upon;

but as we are quite among friends, I will take you in this way, if you will excuse me.'

They entered. Fanny's imagination had prepared her for something grander than a mere spacious, oblong room, fitted up for the purpose of devotion . . . 'I am disappointed,' said she, in a low voice, to Edmund. 'This is not my idea of a chapel. There is nothing awful here, nothing melancholy, nothing grand. Here are no aisles, no arches, no inscriptions, no banners. No banners, cousin, to be "blown by the night wind of Heaven." No signs that a "Scottish monarch sleeps below".'[2]

Jane Austen, *Mansfield Park* (1814)

1 *window tax*. A tax first levied in England in 1696 'for the purpose of defraying the expenses and making up the deficiency arising from clipped and defaced coinage in the recoinage of silver during the reign of William III' (*Encyclopaedia Britannica*). Nearly all inhabited houses were assessed at two shillings a year and tax was added according to the number of windows. The tax was repealed in 1851.

2 *blown by the night wind of Heaven* and *Scottish monarch sleeps below*. These are quotations from Sir Walter Scott's *The Lay of the Last Minstrel*, which was his first important original work.

TITLES

Even in the 21st century, it is courteous to address people correctly. It is less important to get this right than it used to be and nobody is going to think less of you for making a minor slip of titular etiquette. Nevertheless, it is still important to try to get this right.

As a general guideline, the most common title is 'Sir'. This is granted to knights and baronets and, unless you are on first-name terms with them, the correct form of address would be 'Dear Sir Bob'. Sir Bob's wife, on the other hand, would be addressed as 'Dear Lady Charlton' and this would also be her title if she was a peer in her own right.

Bob and Jane Charlton's children should be referred to as 'The Honourable Lancelot and Lucretia' on an envelope but as 'Mr' or 'Miss Family Name' in the letter itself.

A Dame is a woman who has been granted a life peerage. She is not addressed as 'Lady' but as 'Dame', hence, 'Dame Judi Dench'. The next highest rank before a peerage is a baronet and this fellow would also be 'Sir Bob'.

UNTITLED

MAN *Dear Sir, or Dear Mr* **WOMAN** *Dear Madam, Mrs, Miss or Ms* **CHILDREN** *Dear First Name*

RELIGIOUS

ARCHBISHOP *My Lord Archbishop* **BISHOP** *My Lord Bishop*
DEAN *Very Revd Sir* **CLERGY** *Revd Sir*

OTHER PROFESSIONALS

JUDGE *Sir or Madam* **PRIVY COUNCILLORS** *Sir or Madam*
MEMBERS OF PARLIAMENT *Sir or Madam*
DOCTOR *Dear Dr* **SURGEON** *Dear Mr or Ms*

TITLED

DUKE *Dear Duke* **DUCHESS** *Dear Duchess*
MARQUIS *Dear Lord X* **MARCHIONESS** *Dear Lady X*
EARL *Dear Lord* **COUNTESS** *Dear Lady*
VISCOUNT *Dear Lord* **VISCOUNTESS** *Dear Lady*
BARON *Dear Lord* **BARONESS** *Dear Lady or Dear Baroness*
BARONET *Dear Lord* **BARONET'S WIFE** *Dear Lady*
KNIGHT *Sir* **KNIGHT'S WIFE** *Madam*

ILLUSTRATION 4   This basic chart shows how to address people who have specific titles. (For a more complete list of correct styles of address, see the appendix on p.238

MILITARY

Commissioned officers of HM Forces are addressed by rank, together with decorations, if any.

For naval officers, add 'RN'. The main titles, in ranking order, are as follows:

ARMY	AIR FORCE	NAVY
Field Marshal	Marshal of the Royal Air Force	Admiral of the Fleet
General	Air Chief Marshal	Admiral
Lieutenant General	Air Marshal	Vice Admiral
Major General	Air Vice Marshal	Rear Admiral
Brigadier General	Air Commodore	Commodore
Colonel	Group Captain	Captain
Lieutenant-Colonel	Wing Commander	Commander
Major	Squadron Leader	Lieutenant Commander
Captain	Flight Lieutenant	Lieutenant
First Lieutenant	Flying Officer	Sub-Lieutenant
Second Lieutenant	Pilot Officer	

Army officers may have their arm of service added, e.g. RA, RE.

When the woman is military and the man is not, her name comes before his, e.g. Lt-Col. Jane Smith and Mr John Smith.

When they are both in the military, the highest-ranking person's name comes first.

OTHER USEFUL PHRASES

'For the attention of' can be placed underneath the recipient's main address in order that the letter should go straight to a named person within a large organisation. If you then wish to clarify the subject matter, *'Re:'* is a very useful addition between *'Dear Mr X'* and the main text of the letter. Both of these phrases can add clarity, particularly when there is no personal connection between the writer and the recipient.

53 Downs Road
East Shilton
SH17 5PJ

Martin Joggings
Royal and United Alliance
73 Ballpark
Worcs
BR9 3HT

23 September 2003

For the Attention of Martin Joggings

Dear Mr Joggings,

Re: 43 United Front, London SW13

I am writing to you today to . . .

3

G R A M M A R &

PUNCTUATION

- WHY STUDY GRAMMAR?
- PUNCTUATION
- SPELLING
- ABBREVIATIONS
- TIPS ON STYLE

Grammar refers to the set of rules that allow us to combine words in our language into larger units. Some combinations of words are possible in English and some are not, and most native speakers of the language simply use correct grammar without having to think about what they are doing. Any native speaker would automatically say, for example, 'I would really like a cup of tea' and not 'I would a cup of tea really like'.

Nobody taught you to speak this way; you simply absorb it from being exposed to your native language during childhood. The study of grammar, however, enables you to use your language so that the sentence structure may be slightly different, and more interesting, and yet still be correct, and comprehensible, to every reader.

WHY STUDY GRAMMAR?

Studying grammar can help you to write more effectively. It will help you to modify your language and it will help your reader to understand what you are saying. It is easy to look words up in a dictionary or, nowadays, to run your letter through a spellcheck. It is much harder to run a letter through a grammar check. No computer can manipulate the tiny differentials in language that make up correct grammar as effectively as any educated native speaker. It's worth learning grammar because:

1 It helps you to write correctly and therefore to create a good impression.

2 It helps your reader to understand what you are saying and avoids confusion.

3 It helps you to punctuate your letter correctly, again avoiding confusion and misunderstanding.

4 A good grasp of your own grammar makes it far easier to learn a foreign language.

5 It helps you to understand what other people are trying to say in their letters.

THE SENTENCE

A sentence should express one complete thought. It should consist of a string of words beginning with a capital letter and ending with a full stop, although, of course, it could end with a question mark or an exclamation mark. The sentence is made up of the words which are generally referred to by a classification system called Parts of Speech. This describes their function.

NOUNS

A noun is the name of anything: man, woman, England, apple, Manchester United.

There are four kinds of noun in English:

1. Common nouns, which are names that are not specific to particular people or things. They begin with a lower-case letter: writer, newspaper, mountain.

2. Proper nouns, which are the names of specific people, places or occasions and which begin with a capital letter: Charles Dickens, *The Times*, Mount Everest.

3. Abstract nouns, which are the names of qualities, states or activities: laughter, beauty, love.

4. Collective nouns, which are names for a group or collection of similar things: crowd, team, army.

Most plurals of nouns end in an s. There are, however, a number of exceptions.

1. Nouns ending in o, ch, sh, ss or x form their plural by adding es: tomato, tomatoes; box, boxes.

2. Nouns ending in y following a consonant drop the y and add ies: fly, flies; baby, babies.

3. Some nouns ending in f or fe drop the f and add ves: wife, wives; loaf, loaves. (But some do not: roof, roofs.)

4. Some foreign words which retain their original Greek or Latin forms retain their original plural forms:

   Latin: axis, axes; medium, media; stratum, strata.

   Greek: crisis, crises; basis, bases; criterion, criteria.

EXERCISE

Pick out and classify the nouns in the following passage:

About a week subsequently to the incidents above narrated, Miss Temple, who had written to Mr Lloyd, received his answer: it appeared that what he said went to corroborate my account. Miss Temple, having assembled the whole school, announced that inquiry had been made into the charges alleged against Jane Eyre, and that she was most happy to be able to pronounce her completely cleared from every imputation. The teachers then shook hands with me and kissed me and a murmur of pleasure ran through the ranks of my companions.

Thus relieved of a grievous load, I from that hour set to work afresh, resolved to pioneer my way through every difficulty. I toiled hard, and my success was proportionate to my efforts; my memory, not naturally tenacious, improved with practice; exercise sharpened my wits. In a few weeks I was promoted to a higher class; in less than two months I was allowed to commence French and drawing. I learned the first two tenses of the verb Etre, and sketched my first cottage (whose walls, by the way, outrivalled in slope those of the leaning tower of Pisa) on the same day.

Extract from Charlotte Brontë's *Jane Eyre*, chapter 8

ANSWERS

week	*common*	murmur	*abstract*	weeks	*common*
incidents	*common*	pleasure	*abstract*	class	*common*
Miss Temple	*proper*	ranks	*collective*	months	*common*
Mr Lloyd	*proper*	companions	*common*	French	*proper*
answer	*common*	load	*common*	drawing	*common*
account	*common*	hour	*common*	tenses	*abstract*
Miss Temple	*proper*	way	*abstract*	verb	*common*
school	*common*	difficulty	*abstract*	cottage	*common*
inquiry	*common*	success	*abstract*	walls	*common*
charges	*common*	efforts	*abstract*	slope	*common*
Jane Eyre	*proper*	memory	*abstract*	tower	*common*
imputation	*abstract*	practice	*abstract*	Pisa	*proper*
teachers	*common*	exercise	*common*	day	*common*
hands	*common*	wits	*common*		

PRONOUNS

A pronoun is a word used instead of a noun. The most important aspect of the pronoun to note, for practical purposes, is that the only words in the English language which have retained different forms depending on whether they are the subject or the object of a sentence are all pronouns. As a basic guideline the subject of a sentence is the person doing the main action. The object is the person at the receiving end of this action. The difference between the two leads to one of the classic confusions of the English language – the difference in usage between 'I' (subject pronoun) and 'me' (object pronoun).

Nominative (subject form)	Objective (object form)
I	me
he	him
she	her
we	us
they	them
who	whom

☞ **When trying to decide, ask yourself if you would use 'me' in the same sentence on its own. 'John and me went to the party' doesn't sound too bad but 'me went to the party' is wrong.**

EXAMPLE

I am the subject of this sentence. He told me some news about Suzy.

When deciding whether a person is the subject or the object of
a sentence, you must look at the main verb (or doing word) and ask
yourself 'who does this verb refer to?'

EXERCISE

Complete the following sentences with the correct form of the personal
pronoun.

1 John and —— went to the party (I, me).

2 The book was for John and —— (I, me).

ANSWER 1

A Ask yourself 'which is the verb in question 1?'

B Answer: went

C Who went?

D Answer: John and I

ANSWER 2

A Ask yourself 'which is the verb in question 2?'

B Answer: was

C What was?

D Answer: the book – therefore John and me must be the objects
of this sentence

VERBS

It is possible to have a sentence without a verb, but it is unusual.
A verb, as mentioned above, is the 'doing' word in a sentence. It is the
word that drives the sentence along – the 'action' word. It is the part
of speech by which we are able to say what a thing is – for example,
'Spot *is* a dog' – or with which we are able to describe what a person,
animal or thing does – for example, 'Spot *barks* loudly'.

The thing to remember about verbs is that they have certain features which are not shared by other parts of speech. They have different forms to indicate at what time an action happened (past, present or future tenses) and they have different forms to indicate who is doing the action ('I *do*', 'he *does*'.) To get this wrong is, clearly, ungrammatical.

Verbs are either regular or irregular. Regular verbs add 'ed' to form the past tense and, generally, present few problems to the native speaker.

There are, however, over 250 irregular verbs.

EXAMPLE

present	past	past participle
burn	burnt	burnt
saw	sawed	sawn
dream	dreamt	dreamt

Just remember to check if you're not sure. A useful reference book for English grammar is *English Grammar in Use* by Raymond Murphy (Cambridge University Press). A useful website is

WEB TIP   *http://members.nbci.com/, or try **www.studyweb.com***

SPLIT INFINITIVES

This is a very common mistake and you should try to avoid it. 'To boldly go where no man has gone before' is *wrong*. It may sound correct but you should never split the 'to' part of the verb from the main part of the verb ('go') mainly because the meaning of the sentence can then become unclear.

EXAMPLE

wrong: I want to just catch the bus.

right: I just want to catch the bus.

Now we know exactly what you want.

You will see split infinitives in use frequently. No one will cease to communicate with you because you have split an infinitive but it is better – much better – to get these things right.

ADJECTIVES

An adjective is a word that describes a noun or, possibly, another adjective.

EXAMPLE

The car is *dark blue*.

Adjectives can make your letter a little more descriptive or lively but only when used in moderation. In other European languages, the way that the adjective is written must change to agree with the noun it is describing. In English, there are almost no adjectives like this, but a very few have been absorbed from the continent:

EXAMPLE

He is blond. She is blonde.

ADVERBS

Adverbs describe verbs and adjectives and the majority of adverbs are formed by adding 'ly' to the end of the corresponding adjective.

EXAMPLE

He ran quickly.

Adverbs are, in general, the first signs of over-written prose. If you need to shorten your letter, try cutting out any extraneous adverbs.

PREPOSITIONS AND CONJUNCTIONS

Prepositions are the little words which are used with nouns to show the relation in which these nouns stand to some other word in the sentence.

EXAMPLE

The horse is *in* the stable.

It is usually better not to end a sentence with a preposition. This is called a hanging preposition and tends to look rather inelegant. In casual prose, however, it is perfectly acceptable.

EXAMPLE

wrong: This is the moment I've been waiting *for*.

right: This is the moment for which I've been waiting.

Occasionally it is difficult to choose the correct preposition since several are acceptable in spoken language. Here is a guide to the most commonly mistaken prepositions:

afflict	*with*	**equal**	*to*
agree	*to* (something)	**guilty**	*of*
agree	*with* (somebody)	**opposite**	*to*
complain	*of*	**prevail**	*on*
different	*from* (US *than*)	**protest**	*against*
disappointed	*in* (something)	**similar**	*to*
disappointed	*with* (somebody)	**tired**	*of* (something)
disgusted	*at/by* (something)	**tired**	*with* (action)
disgusted	*with* (somebody)	**thirst**	*for*
dislike	*for*	**vexed**	*at* (something)
divide	*amoung* (many)	**vexed**	*with* (somebody)
divide	*between* (two)		

Conjunctions are the little words that join a word with another part of the sentence: and, but, or.

It is unusual, though not impossible, to start a sentence with 'and', but this should only be the case when you want to emphasise the fact that you are doing so.

PUNCTUATION

The rules for punctuation are conventions that have been developed through the centuries by printers and publishers and are simply devices for making written text easier to read and understand. Punctuation helps the reader to make sense of a large piece of written communication by breaking it down into smaller, more manageable, sections. It also helps to make the appearance of the written page clearer and more attractive. In speech, we can use gestures, give emphasis to a word, or raise and lower our voices to help illustrate our meaning. In written work, much of this stress and clarification must be accomplished by punctuation.

Some conventions of punctuation are obligatory and some are optional, but they should all be used with discretion and good common sense. Sentences may be rendered meaningless by lack of punctuation, or they may take on an entirely different meaning, and you should always attempt to use the correct punctuation.

THE FULL STOP

This is probably the most straightforward aspect of punctuation. The full stop is used to separate one sentence from another. When you come to the end of a sentence, you use a full stop. If no full stops were used, a piece of text would be almost impossible to read or would mean something else entirely.

EXAMPLE

The king walked around the castle an hour after his head was chopped off.

The king walked around the castle. An hour after, his head was chopped off.

The full stop may also be used after abbreviations such as B.A., H.M. and Co., but is omitted if the shortened word includes the last letter of the word, e.g. Dr, Mr and Ltd.

THE COMMA

The comma lies at the place in the sentence where you would normally take a breath, or where there is a natural pause. It is the most frequently used punctuation mark and has many functions. It is generally used:

1 To record a list of things:

   At the party we had cake, jelly, ice-cream, biscuits and fizzy drinks.

2 To mark out direct speech:

   'So tell me,' he said, 'do you come here often?'

3 To mark off a sentence or clause where a pause is needed in reading:

   Among the people who came to my party were the actor, John Brown, and his wife, Susie Smith, who wrote the film we had been to see earlier, and her friend Jim.

4 To mark off words like however, therefore and of course.

Generally speaking, and particularly in business prose, you do not need a comma before 'and' or 'but', although it is better to insert one if it will make the sentence more readily comprehensible.

THE SEMI-COLON

The semi-colon is used to join two grammatically complete sentences that are related in subject matter. If you wish to join these two, separate thoughts in one sentence, you will need to use a semi-colon. Another way to think of this principle is that you need a semi-colon when you require a slightly longer pause than you would have with a comma, but where you do not want to break the line of thought as you would do if you were to use a full stop.

It can also be used where you make a long list of items, all of which require further identification with a comma:

Among the people present at the theatre were the actress, Lizzie Brown, wife of the author; Jack Black, the author; Harry Grey, the producer and John Smith, a fan.

This would clearly be incomprehensible without the semi-colons.

THE COLON

The colon is generally used before a list or to introduce a quotation:

He offered me various things for my birthday: a CD, a book, a blue teapot and a pair of earrings.

THE EXCLAMATION MARK

The exclamation mark is used after an interjection, an exclamatory sentence or an expression of great feeling. It is therefore used to express a sudden moment of passionate feeling, whether this be surprise or joy. It is generally over-used in social letters and should be avoided when not strictly necessary. Do not use an exclamation mark without first asking yourself: 'Does this sentence really deserve one?'

> ☞ **Too many exclamation marks in any piece of writing trivialise it by making it seem hysterical.**

It can, however, be very useful if you are making a statement that might be considered a little forward when addressed to people you do not know very well. It can make written text seem more relaxed and informal.

I had a really marvellous time!

Thanks for the toy rocket!

THE QUESTION MARK

A question mark is used after a direct question but not after an indirect one:

'When are you going on holiday?' I asked him.

I asked him when he was going on holiday.

Bear in mind that question marks replace full stops. Since question marks normally mark the end of a sentence, a comma should not normally be required.

INVERTED COMMAS

Inverted commas are used to enclose direct speech or to enclose an extract or quotation. The extra punctuation will be inside the quotation marks if the sentence quoted is complete:

She told me, 'We really like France.'

Here, for example, 'We really like France' is a complete sentence in itself, so the full stop goes inside the quotation marks. Compare:

When I asked her, she said 'blue'.

The word 'blue' does not form a complete sentence so the full stop goes outside the inverted commas.

If the quotation is indented, it is not necessary to use quotation marks since the layout already indicates that this is direct speech.

If the quotation ends the sentence, then a full stop, a question mark or an exclamation mark is placed before the final quotation mark.

If the question mark belongs to the sentence as a whole, and not to the direct speech, then the question mark goes outside:

Did he say, 'It is against my beliefs'?

If you are going to use a quotation within direct speech, you should use double quotation marks to mark off the quotation in order to differentiate it from the direct speech:

'Well,' he said, 'I guess that nobody wants to hear me read "Men are from Pluto" then?'

THE APOSTROPHE

This is probably the most abused of all forms of punctuation. No one will take your business letter seriously if you cannot master its use.

There are two main, and quite separate, uses for the apostrophe.

1 It is used to denote possession:

   The boy's football

   My mother's bag

2 It is also used to show the omission of a letter or letters:

   I've been to the shops.

   What's on my sister's T-shirt?

Never confuse the two.

When in doubt, ask yourself if the object in question belongs to anybody. This is not complicated. The football belongs to the boy. The bag belongs to the mother.

Most confusion arises out of the word *its*, meaning *belonging to it*. It is occasionally confused with *it's*, which is an abbreviation of the two words *it is* or *it has*. The abbreviation in *it's* merely indicates the absence of the letter 'i' .

Ask yourself: can this word be replaced by 'it is' or 'it has'?

If it cannot, then it *must* be *its* without an apostrophe.

EXAMPLE

The cat scratched its leg. (no apostrophe)

The cat is not there. It's a shame.

Always remember when dealing with a possessive plural to put the apostrophe before the final s unless the plural word itself ends in an *s*. This sounds more complicated than it is.

The people's party was better than the children's party.

The adults' party was better than the teenagers' party.

Just ask yourself: whose party was it?

The people – so it is the party of the people.

The adults – so it is the party of the adults.

In other words the apostrophe goes at the end of the collective word.

> ☞ **Possessive pronouns (its, hers, theirs) never take apostrophes.**

BRACKETS

These are used when you need to add something to a sentence to clarify its meaning but which bears no direct relevance to the sentence itself. If you could adequately use commas instead, then use commas: they look neater and they indicate that you have a correct grasp of grammar.

Square brackets tend to indicate an omission in the text or something scientific. You should not normally need them in letter writing.

DASHES AND HYPHENS

A dash is a long line which is often used instead of a comma or a semi-colon:

The boys – always in a hurry – ran for the bus.

A hyphen is a shorter line which is used to join two words when they would make more sense as one word:

self-discipline

second-hand

The primary function of the hyphen is to indicate that two or more words are to be read together as a single word with its own meaning. The hyphen is always used in phrasal compounds such as *stick-in-the-mud*. Some hyphenated words are in a constant state of flux. Fifty years ago, *today* and *tomorrow* were very often hyphenated while *son in law* was not. If in doubt, look in a dictionary but, in general, if a hyphen will clarify the meaning of a word, use one.

Many hyphenated words are only hyphenated if they are adjectival (i.e. form a single phrase with a specific descriptive meaning). 'The ankle-deep mud' (attributive) is technically correct, but there is nothing wrong with the phrase 'the mud is ankle deep' (predicative).

You hyphenate words in order to join them together so that they have a new, specialised meaning different from each word's individual meaning when used independently.

Think about 'the old-fashioned dresser'. The 'old, fashioned dresser' would be a dresser that is both antique and highly decorated. The 'old-fashioned dresser' is a dresser that has gone right out of fashion.

EXERCISE

Insert the correct punctuation into the following three paragraphs:

1 here is the video I promised to bring you said luke what is it called asked tom see for yourself replied luke

2 where are you going for your holidays asked sophie we are going to new york answered beatrice you cant go there exclaimed sophie why not asked beatrice because its too far replied sophie

3 do you think youll win the match my father asked well I think its very likely I replied it doesnt really matter as long as you do your best said my father

ANSWERS

1 'Here is the video I promised to bring you,' said Luke.

 'What is it called?' asked Tom.

 'See for yourself,' replied Luke.

2 'Where are you going for your holidays?' asked Sophie.

 'We are going to New York,' answered Beatrice.

 'You can't go there!' exclaimed Sophie.

 'Why not?' asked Beatrice.

 'Because it's too far,' replied Sophie.

3 'Do you think you'll win the match?' my father asked.

 'Well, I think it's very likely,' I replied.

 'It doesn't really matter, as long as you do your best,'
 said my father.

SPELLING

The English language contains around half a million different words,
while French has around 100,000; Russian approximately 150,000 and
German about 200,000. Most of us use only around 15–20,000 of these
words on a regular basis.

> ☞ If in doubt, always consult a good dictionary. Keep one handy.

Our vocabulary is enormous because English is essentially a mixture of
two separate language systems: the system used in England before the
Norman Conquest in 1066 and the system used after this date when
a new written language was devised by the Norman-French invaders.
English has, in addition, incorporated large numbers of other foreign
words along the way. This means, in effect, that English often contains
two or three different synonyms (different words meaning the same
thing) to express one concept – all drawn from quite different language

systems. Some spellings were changed to bring words nearer to the form they had in other languages and the changes introduced letters that have never been pronounced in English – the *b* in debt, for example, or the *l* in salmon.

English spellings have generally remained fixed, while pronunciation has changed radically. During the Middle Ages it was perfectly permissible to spell the same word in several different ways. It was only in the late 15th century, when the first printers introduced their new trade into England, that a new, standardised system was felt to be necessary.

Another problem is that English contains around forty different basic sounds, not including all the foreign sounds that have been incorporated into the language, but only twenty-six letters with which to represent them on paper. So many letter combinations have to double for different sounds, adding to the confusion.

Despite all this, spelling is important. It creates a good impression and makes your letter easily comprehensible. It's a shame to start off well and then ruin the whole thing by slipping up on a small but truly irritating error.

Bad spelling annoys people – and can, occasionally, lead to misunderstandings. Follow some basic guidelines and you will, usually, get it right. Again, it's worth the effort.

BASIC SPELLING RULES

1   i before e except after c, when they make the sound 'ee', for example:

	fierce	niece	relieve
but	ceiling	deceive	receive

2   When al- is added as a prefix at the beginning of a word to make a new word, it is spelt with one l, for example:

al+ready becomes already

al+though becomes although

al+together becomes altogether

3   Do not add or subtract letters when you add a prefix,
    for example:

    un+easy becomes uneasy

    un-necessary becomes unnecessary

4   Consonants double after a short vowel, for example:

    tap becomes tapping

    beg becomes begging

    hop becomes hopping

5   Drop the final e before a suffix beginning with a vowel,
    for example:

    abbreviate+ion becomes abbreviation

    argue +able becomes arguable

    fascinate+ing becomes fascinating

    except after -ce or -ge, for example:

    change+able becomes changeable

    courage+ous becomes courageous

    outrage+ous becomes outrageous

6   Generally, double a final consonant when adding a suffix
    beginning with a vowel, for example:

    stop+ed becomes stopped

    win+er becomes winner

7   The suffix -ful is always spelt with one l, for example:

    faithful   grateful   hopeful

8 When an ending which begins with a vowel is added to a word which ends in a single vowel plus a consonant, the consonant is doubled if the stress is on the end of the word or if the word has only one part, for example:

admit+ance becomes admittance

begin+ing becomes beginning

equip+ed becomes equipped

9 When the adverb ending ly is added to an adjective which ends in an -le, then the -le is usually dropped, for example:

gentle+ly becomes gently

idle+ly becomes idly

subtle+ly becomes subtly

10 When an ending is added to a word which ends in a consonant plus y, the y changes into i (unless the new ending already begins with an i), for example:

beauty+ful becomes beautiful

carry+age becomes carriage

11 When an ending which begins with a vowel is added to a word which ends in a single vowel plus l, then the l is doubled, for example:

cancel+ation becomes cancellation

excel+ent becomes excellent

equip+ed becomes equipped

12 When an ending which begins with e, i or y is added to a word which ends in c, a k is also added to the c to keep its hard sound, for example:

panic+ing becomes panicking

13 When the adjective suffix -ous or -ary is added to a word which ends in -our, the u of the -our is dropped, for example:

glamour+ous becomes glamorous

humour+ous becomes humorous

14 The plural of a word which ends in a consonant y is formed by changing the y to i and adding -es, for example:

accessory becomes accessories

diary becomes diaries

15 The plural of a word which ends in a vowel plus y is made by adding s, for example:

jersey+s becomes jerseys

journey+s becomes journeys

16 The plural of a word which ends in -eau is made by adding s or x, for example:

bureau becomes bureaux

gateau becomes gateaux

17 The plural of a word which ends in s, x, z, sh or ch is made by adding -es, for example:

bus becomes buses

focus becomes focuses

OTHER AIDS TO SPELLING

A common type of spelling error is to run words together by writing two words as one. Always write these phrases as separate words:

a lot	in fact
all right	just as
even if	no one
even though	of course

In some cases, the spelling depends on the meaning. For example, write 'nobody' as one word when it is a synonym of 'no person', but write 'no body' as two words when meaning 'there is no corpse in the mortuary'.

HOMOPHONES

A homophone is a word which is pronounced in the same way as another word but which has a different meaning. This inevitably leads to spelling confusion. Think about which of the words it is that you really want to use before you write that word down. Here is a list of the most commonly mistaken homophones or words that are not strictly homophones but which sound so similar that they are frequently confused:

accept	except	cereal	serial
access	excess	coarse	course
advice	advise	conscience	conscious
affect	effect	council	counsel
aid	aide	decent	descent
aisle	isle	desert	dessert
altar	alter	device	devise
assistance	assistants	dual	duel
ate	eight	elicit	illicit
bare	bear	emigrate	migrate
beer	bier	eminent	imminent
brake	break	envelop	envelope
business	busyness	fair	fare
buy	by	father	farther
canvas	canvass	formally	formerly

forth	fourth		principal	principle
grate	great		read	red
heard	herd		right	wright
idle	idol		seed	cede
ingenious	ingenuous		sole	soul
lessen	lesson		stationary	stationery
loose	lose		to	too
maize	maze		wander	wonder
miner	minor		wave	waive
of	off		way	weigh
pain	pane		weather	whether
passed	past		were	where
personal	personnel		which	witch
precede	proceed		wood	would

COMMON CONFUSIONS

Be particularly careful with your use of the words 'were' and 'where'
and 'their' and 'there', which tend to cause particular problems and are
considered really fundamental errors.

CONFUSION OF 'THEIR' AND 'THERE' 'Their' is a possessive word
and is always followed by a noun, e.g. their book, their clothes, their
friends. 'There' is used either as an adverb meaning 'in that place',
or as a word having no meaning of its own but used along with a verb,
e.g. there was no hope; there is a God.

CONFUSION OF 'WERE' AND 'WHERE' 'Were' is a verb: we were
in the house. 'Where' is an adverb meaning 'in that place' or 'in what
place?', e.g. the house where I grew up.

CONFUSION BETWEEN 'OF' AND 'OFF' 'Of' c...
'belonging to', 'on account of' and 'out of', e.g. one
the father of the bride.'Off' can mean 'away', 'away f...
and the opposite of 'on', e.g. run off; he got off his bike.

CONFUSION OF 'TO', 'TOO' AND 'TWO' 'To' is used to in...
movement towards something, e.g. I ran to him. 'To' is also used to
indicate the infinite of a verb, e.g. I failed to catch him. 'Too' means
more than enough, e.g. he asked too many questions. 'Two' is a number,
e.g. I won two prizes.

CONFUSION BETWEEN 'ITS' AND 'IT'S' As explained above, this
confusion is easily remedied. Remember that 'its' means belonging to
something, e.g. its teeth, its leg, while 'it's' is the shortened form of
'it is', e.g. I think it's raining.

EXERCISE

Which spellings are correct?

1   If (there, their) is another sound I shall be very angry.

2   Please wait (there, their).

3   The girls wore (there, their) darkest shades.

4   Despite all (there, their) efforts, they lost the race.

5   She is the older (of, off) the two.

6   He went (of, off) to fetch the book.

7   The wall was (to, too, two) high to climb.

8   The (to, too, two) robbers were (to, too, two) shaken to escape.

9   We went (to, too, two) close (to, too, two) the edge.

10 The kangaroo can jump (its, it's) own height.

11 I shall know when (its, it's) the right time.

12 The leopard cannot change (its, it's) spots.

ANSWERS

1 there

2 there

3 their

4 their

5 of

6 off

7 too

8 two, too

9 too, to

10 its

11 it's

12 its

A NOTE ON AMERICAN ENGLISH

American English has attempted to simplify and shorten British English. Reformers included Isaac Pitman (who later invented shorthand) and Mark Twain. The American Philological Association was established in 1876, but it was when the Scots-American millionaire Andrew Carnegie (of Carnegie Hall fame) gave $250,000 to the cause some thirty years later that it really took off.

Words with alternative spellings then officially had the longer one declared invalid so that, in American dictionaries, *judgement* is now spelt *judgment*, while *axe* is *ax* and *programme* has become *program*. The most frequent use of American spelling in English is the gradual mutation of the ending *-ise* into the ending *-ize*. Most words in this category can now be spelt either way, and each is equally acceptable, but for just a few it is imperative to stick to the *-ise* ending. Anything else is wrong. Here they are:

advertise	demise	exercise	reprise
advise	despise	exorcise	revise
apprise	devise	franchise	rise
arise	disenfranchise	improvise	supervise
chastise	disguise	incise	surmise
circumcise	enfranchise	merchandise	surprise
comprise	enterprise	mortise	televise
compromise	excise	premise	

ABBREVIATIONS

The following are lists of abbreviations in common use. (Some full stops are frequently omitted in printed matter, e.g. BA, UN.)

ABBREVIATIONS USED BEFORE A PERSON'S NAME

Capt.	Captain
Col.	Colonel
Dr	Doctor
Gen.	General
H.M.	His/Her Majesty
H.R.H.	Her Royal Highness/His Royal Highness
Lieut. or Lt.	Lieutenant
Maj.	Major
P.C.	Police Constable
Prof.	Professor
Revd	Reverend

ABBREVIATIONS USED AFTER A PERSON'S NAME

B.A.	Bachelor of Arts
B.Sc.	Bachelor of Science
J.P.	Justice of the Peace
M.A.	Master of Arts
M.D.	Doctor of Medicine
M.P.	Member of Parliament
LL.B.	Bachelor of Laws
Ph.D.	Doctor of Philosophy
Q.C.	Queen's Counsel
R.N.	Royal Navy

OTHER USEFUL ABBREVIATIONS

A.A.	Automobile Association
a.m.	Before noon
B.C.	Before Christ
G.M.T.	Greenwich Mean Time
i.e.	*id est* – that is
R.S.V.P	Please reply
U.N.	United Nations
v	*versus* – against
viz.	namely

TIPS ON STYLE

END-FOCUS

It is normal to arrange the information in our letters so that the most important information comes at the end. The beginning of a sentence tends to convey the more general information, or the information that is obvious from the context. Changing this sentence structure will subtly change the focus of your sentence.

Compare:

The British public is not interested in foreign policy.

Foreign policy does not interest the British public.

The difference in emphasis is very subtle, but if you say the two sentences out loud, you will hear a slight but noticeable shift in meaning.

FRONT-FOCUS

Using the principle of regular sentence structure and end-focus, we can make an expression much more conspicuous by shifting it. It is very unusual for a verb or the object of a sentence to come before its subject. Give them front-focus, therefore, and they will really make an impression:

Cannabis they used occasionally, but cocaine they never touched.

Readily available were the drugs in that part of the country.

END-WEIGHT

It is normal in a sentence for the longer part to come at the end. It is much more difficult to understand a sentence if it has a very long opening clause.

clumsy: The rate at which young girls these days are eating junk food and then dieting like mad in order to work away its calorific ill-effects is the real problem.

better: The real problem is the rate at which young girls these days are eating junk food and then dieting like mad in order to work away its calorific ill-effects.

MISPLACED EXPRESSIONS AND WORDS

Think about where you place the words in a written sentence, since this can alter its meaning radically. The classic example of this is the word 'only', which refers merely to the word following it, thus making it crucial to place it before the correct word.

Compare:

Only I told them that the meeting was postponed.

I *only* told them that the meeting was postponed.

I told *only* them that the meeting was postponed.

I told them *only* that the meeting was postponed.

I told them that *only* the meeting was postponed.

I told them that the *only* meeting was postponed.

I told them that the meeting was *only* postponed.

> ☞ 'Less' signifies an abstract number of items. 'Fewer' signifies a specific, quantifiable number of items. The two words are not interchangeable. 'I have less hair than you.' 'You have fewer hats than me.'

LONGWINDEDNESS

Some phrases with general words such as '*fact*' are more elegant, and more readily comprehensible, when they are replaced by simpler conjugations or prepositions. For example:

✗ I went with my sister to see the film in spite of the fact that I don't really like horror films.

would be better left simply as:

✔ I went with my sister to see the film even though I don't really like horror films.

Other related, and improvable, phrases include:

longwinded	*better*
on account of the fact	because
due to the fact that	because
apart from the fact that	except
as a consequence of	because of
during the course of	during

> ☞ Collective nouns take singular verbs, e.g. 'The flock of sheep is expanding.' It is the flock which is expanding, not the sheep themselves.

UNNECESSARY OR REPEATED SOUNDS

Avoid putting words near each other if they sound the same or almost the same but have different meanings. It can be quite confusing to read and, in any event, looks peculiar.

✗ At this point I should point out that I am still busy working on my essay.

✔ I should now mention that I am still busy working on my essay.

It couldn't be easier to spot an error like this, so make sure that you do something about it when you see one.

It is possible, also, to improve a sentence by rephrasing it to omit a pronoun:

 unnecessary: **In my book it says that the use of pronouns is simple.**

 clearer: **My book says that the use of pronouns is simple.**

PRONOUN AGREEMENT

Remember that pronouns must agree with the subject they are replacing.

 Get *a new* car because *they* run better.

 Get *a new* car because *it* will run better.

There is only one car involved – remember to use a singular form.

TENSE CONSISTENCY

Be consistent in your use of tenses.

If you go to the shop first thing in the morning (*present tense*), you could buy everything you need (*conditional*).

When you go to the shop first thing in the morning (*present*), you can buy everything you need (*present*).

4

PERSONAL
LETTERS

- PRESENTATION
- APOLOGIES
- WRITING TO CHILDREN
- CONDOLENCES & CONGRATULATIONS
- FAN MAIL
- GENERAL FRIENDSHIP
- LOVE LETTERS
- POLITE REQUESTS & RUDE LETTERS

The skills of personal letter writing have been heavily eroded by other, more modern forms of communication, but social correspondence still remains a very intimate form of letter writing and provides far more opportunity for considered reflection than a telephone call and far more opportunity for description than an email.

A letter can show you at your best as well as giving you the means to express yourself in a much more sensitive way than would be possible with speech. Despite this intimacy, however, presentation is still very important – even if you are writing to a friend or relative.

PRESENTATION

Generally speaking, social letters should always be handwritten. This is because a personal letter should convey personal thoughts and the more impersonal the format in which it is written, the less impact your letter will have.

Always bear in mind the need to write as clearly and neatly as possible – there's no point going to all that effort if no one can read what you have written. This is particularly important with sensitive, social communications, since if you are reading news of a long-lost relative or a declaration of love, you do not want to have to decipher it. You want to be able to relish the information itself rather than requiring three days merely to decode it. It is, naturally, unforgivable to word-process such personal correspondence as a letter of condolence. It would totally defeat the purpose of writing the letter.

Remember to add the date and the address from which you are writing. The recipient may wish to reply and even if your current whereabouts are obvious to you, they may not be so to your reader.

When writing to old people or to children, remember to use particularly clear handwriting and, if at all possible, slightly larger letters than normal. People with fading eyesight will appreciate this and children will simply find it easier to read. Children also like the written word to be broken up with pictures so, even if you think you can't draw, any illustrations, cartoons or photos will add to the enjoyment.

Here are some guidelines and samples of the most common forms of personal letters.

APOLOGIES

Admitting that you have behaved badly is never easy and, in many ways, the handwritten letter is the most acceptable way to deal with the situation. The effort that you have put into the work demonstrates, to some extent, the contrition that you may feel. Bear in mind that your letter should always be as short as possible and to the point, and that trying to incorporate further excuses simply makes you look pathetic and might even make the situation worse.

On a practical note, it may be easier to say 'sorry' in a letter than over the telephone, since you may not wish actually to speak to the person to whom the apology is addressed. 'Sorry' is one of the most prized words in the English language and when people hear it they are often willing to forgive a great deal of earlier discomfort.

LOUISA GENDER, 53 DOWNS ROAD,
EAST SHILTON, SH17 5PJ

George Simons
42 Mansfield Street
Jessopton
Leics.
JS3 4TY

22 September 2003

Dear George,

I am so sorry.

I know that's not good enough and that you probably don't want to hear from me right now, but I just wanted you to know how profoundly sorry I am.

I respect your right not to reply to this letter but I hope you feel that you can.

Yours,

Louisa

LUKE GENDER, 53 DOWNS ROAD,
EAST SHILTON, SH17 5PJ

Akash Kamerkar
12 Mansfield Street
Jessopton
Leics. JS5 2TY

22 September 2003

Dear Akash,

I'm so sorry that I was rude to you at the meeting. It was careless and stupid of me. I could try and say that I was over-tired because of the project and that my lumbago was causing me enormous pain, but that would really be just more excuses and I don't want to make my blunder any worse.

I hope you can forget what I said and that it won't affect our working relationship or our friendship. I don't know what came over me and I am truly sorry.

Sincerely,

Luke

Akash may not reply to this letter but at least you know that you have come clean and done your best. If you are writing a letter of apology, apologise!

WRITING TO CHILDREN

Letters to children should also be as clear as possible. They should not be patronising but neither should they use over-complicated vocabulary. Think about the age of your prospective audience and try to remember how excited you would have been to receive a letter at that age. Then try to live up to those expectations.

DOROTHY GENDER, 53 DOWNS ROAD,
EAST SHILTON, SH17 5PJ

Sophie Simons
42 Mansfield Street
Jessopton
Leics.
JS3 4TY

22 September 2003

Dear Sophie,

Thank you so much for the lovely photo of you and the cats. At the hospital, I put it on the bedside table and every time I plucked a grape, there were you and Tibby and Totty, staring at me in such a cute way. Now that I'm home at last, I've put the photo on top of the hi-fi and I look at it whenever I feel a bit glum. It really cheers me up.

I hope you got everything you wanted for your birthday. I know you really wanted a Playstation, so please let me know if you didn't get one. If that is the case, I will try to buy you one for Christmas instead.

Anyway, I hope school's not too boring and that you haven't got too much homework.

Give the cats a kiss from me.

Love

Aunt Dorothy

Children always want to know facts and are not, generally, interested in things that might happen. If you are writing to suggest a birthday treat, or something similar, make sure that your suggestion is a concrete one – and one that you can actually put into effect. Remember to write as neatly as possible and with quite large gaps between words. If your letter is difficult to read, a child will simply not bother. Likewise, think carefully about your wording – a letter that uses old-fashioned or out-of-date vocabulary will simply label you an old fogey and will not obtain much of a response. Also, try not to be too soppy.

IRENE FEATHERS, 96 GLEBE STREET,
HORNCRUST HILL, BUCKS. BU29 1UP

Bruno Wilson
83 Mansfield Street
Jessopton
Leics JS12 2TY

22 September 2000

Dear Bruno,

I am so sorry to hear from Hugo that you have chicken pox. It must be really horrible for you, particularly since this means that you will miss the trip to the Science Museum.

Hugo will let me know as soon as you are back at school and feeling better. We would really like to organise our own alternative trip to the museum as soon as you are well. I hope that's really soon.

We both miss you.

Love,

Irene

(Hugo's mother)

This is not a letter a modern writer would wish to copy, but it is worth reading and studying. Note the sincerity and passion of the feelings, as well as the style, which is old-fashioned, of course, but remains lucid and simple without being in any way patronising.

My precious Annie,

I take advantage of your gracious permission to write to you, and there is no telling how far my feelings might carry me were I not limited by the conveyance . . . and which must go in this morning's mail. But my limited time does not diminish my affection for you, Annie, nor prevent my thinking of you and wishing for you. I long to see you through the dilatory nights. At dawn when I rise, and all day, my thoughts revert to you in expressions that you cannot hear or I repeat. I hope you will always appear to me as you are now painted on my heart, and that you will endeavour to improve and so conduct yourself as to make you happy and me joyful all our lives. Diligent and earnest attention to all your duties can only accomplish this. I am told you are growing very tall, and I hope very straight. I do not know what the Cadets will say if the Superintendent's children do not practice what he demands of them. They will naturally say he had better attend to his own before he corrects other people's children, and as he permits his to stoop it is hard he will not allow them. You and Agnes must not, therefore, bring me into discredit with my young friends, or give them reason to think that I require more of them than of my own.

I presume your mother has told all about us, our neighbours and our affairs. And indeed she may have done that and not said much either, so far as I know. But we are all well and have much to be grateful for. Tomorrow we anticipate the pleasure of your brother's company, which is always a source of pleasure to us. It is the only time we see him, except when the Corps come under my view at some of their exercises, when my eye is sure to distinguish him among his comrades and follow him over the plain.

Give much love to your dear grandmother, grandfather, Agnes, Miss Sue, Lucretia, and all friends, including the servants. Write sometimes, and think always of your

Affectionate father,

R. E. Lee

Robert E. Lee, US Confederate General, to Anne Lee (1853)

CONDOLENCES & CONGRATULATIONS

These can be particularly difficult. You will want to be as sincere as possible but with an undercurrent of sensitivity suggesting that you know that nothing you say can possibly be of any real assistance. Letters of condolence should include:

- sympathy

- comfort

- offers of practical help – wherever possible

- suggestions of normality – things you might do when the bereaved is feeling better

- tact – avoiding painful subjects and issues

- religious sensitivity

Given that the mere act of writing is the point of the exercise, there are a few pitfalls which you should make sure you avoid.

BAD EXAMPLE

Dear Liz,

We were really shocked to hear about Derek. I had known him even longer than you and I know there is nothing we can say that could possibly make this appalling loss any better. None the less, we wanted to write and say how genuinely shocked and sorry we are.

Your husband was a lovely man, who really didn't deserve all the suffering he went through over the last few months. We will honestly miss his company terribly. We had a super night at The Tavern on Wednesday – I know Derek liked it there and after a few rounds of pool, I could understand why! Anyway, I know there's nothing we can do now but please let us know if you feel like a night out. The drinks are on us!

See you soon,
Lucy

There are clearly a number of things wrong with the above letter.

UNSUITABLE PHRASES Try to avoid words like 'honestly' which are fine in speech but sound very defensive on paper.

TACTLESSNESS This is a very bad time to remind Sophie that you went out with Derek before she did. He was her husband and she is the primary bereaved person here. Respect her seniority in the grief stakes.

HEAVY-HANDEDNESS The mention of his long illness is now unnecessary and irrelevant. It will only add to Sophie's grief and will not bring her any comfort.

SINGLE ISSUE Do not move on to other topics – Sophie does not want to know your thoughts about the state of the pool table at The Tavern, or anywhere else, right now.

HUMOUR Not the time for a joke – even if it's a well-intentioned one. If she does ring and wants to go out, then pay for the drinks without making a fuss. It is, in any event, inappropriately early to be suggesting a night out – unless she suggests it first herself.

GOOD EXAMPLE

Dear Liz,

We were so sorry to hear that Derek has died. We wanted to write and offer our sincere sympathy as soon as we heard.

Your husband was a lovely man, whose company we shall miss tremendously. If there is anything that we can do over the next few weeks, please do let us know - even if it's just to come round with some supper when you don't feel like cooking.

We hope to see you soon - we are thinking of you.

Kind regards,

Lucy

In condolence letters, it's often helpful to mention something lovely that you remember about the deceased – their sense of humour, their kindness or a particular incident that stays in your mind but that the deceased's family may not know about: 'Your father was especially kind to young people – he gave me some really useful advice about dating before I went to university. I can't say it did me much good but it made me laugh at the time!'

SYMPATHY

Expressions of sympathy that are not related to condolence may also often most appropriately be conveyed by a letter to which there is no need for an immediate response. Miscarriage, for example, or a friend's divorce. There are all sorts of occasions when the recipient of the letter might want, or need, time to reply, or when no reply is required. It is best to be as specific as possible without dwelling too heavily on the incident in question. Just show that you are thinking about the person and that you care. When he feels a bit better, he will certainly remember the people who remembered him.

NEWS OF A DIVORCE

Dear Laura,

I was so sorry to hear about your divorce. I have known both of you for such a long time, it seems incredible that you aren't together any more.

I know that I met you through Barry but I just wanted to write and tell you that I'm thinking about you and that there's no question of 'taking sides'. It must be a horrible thing to have to live through.

You are both my friends and I hope that you will continue to be so as I have always valued your friendship. Please feel free to ring me if I can help you in any way.

Yours,
Meg

EXAM FAILURE

Dear Tina,

I was so sorry to hear that you won't be going to medical school in September. You must be very disappointed.

I'm sure you will want to try again next year. I have heard from your Dad that you are going to retake the chemistry next summer and that, in the meantime, you have got a job as a porter at The Clinic. That seems like a really sensible plan of action. I hope you are enjoying it and that you are not too down-hearted.

I do hope you'll come and see us soon, anyway, whatever you decide to do.

Lots of love,

Uncle Bertie

FAILED BUSINESS

Dear Bob,

I was so sorry to hear that your business didn't work out, particularly after all the long hours and effort that you put in. If commitment and energy were what counted, yours would surely have been the most successful business in Hartlepool.

Knowing you, I'm sure you are blaming yourself now, but it was terribly bad luck with interest rates rising as soon as you borrowed the money and then the petrol strike coming out of the blue. It was a brilliant idea and you really deserved to succeed. Please don't get depressed about this. I'm sure it will just be a blip in your brilliant career - it was a really impressive idea and deserved to make you a million.

I feel sure that the next one will.

Best wishes

Ferdinand

CONGRATULATIONS

A good deal will depend on the nature of your relationship with the parties involved. You might be writing on the occasion of an engagement, the birth of a baby or a promotion at work. Bear in mind the appropriate level of intimacy when composing this letter. Try to avoid being over-intimate, but also try to keep the mood casual. If the note is addressed to someone you only know in a professional capacity, do be particularly careful with your phraseology. When writing birth and wedding congratulations, always remember to address them to both of the partners involved.

PASSING DRIVING TEST

Dear Simon

Well done, mate! I was delighted to hear from your sister that you passed your driving test last week. Now you'll really be going places!

It seems like ages since I last saw you. Once you've bought yourself a car, it'll be a whole lot easier to get together. Do give us a ring and let me know how you're fixed up over the next few weeks. It will be great to see you.

All the best,

Patrick

NEW BIRTH

Dear Lulu and Henry,

Congratulations.

I am thrilled for you both and hope to meet Baby X as soon as possible. I will give you a ring when things have quietened down to try and sort out a suitable time.

In the meantime, I hope that Lulu is feeling well and that you are all getting some sleep.

Lots of love, Pat

ENGAGEMENT

Dear Pamela and Tommy,

I was delighted to read about your engagement in the Daily Telegraph yesterday and I hope to meet Tommy some day soon.

Please send my best regards to your parents, Pamela - they must be absolutely thrilled.

Congratulations.

Love,

Jane

FAN MAIL

This will entirely depend on the nature of the appreciation and is also a question of tone. When writing fan mail, remember to bear in mind several crucial points. When you are writing to someone you know to say, for example, how much you enjoyed reading their book, think about how well you know that person and whether they are likely to be surprised or embarrassed by your letter. If this is the case, make sure that your letter is not too personal. Appreciation without cringeworthiness is probably the tone to aim for.

When writing to a complete stranger, possibly a celebrity, to say how much you enjoyed their role in a film, for example, bear in mind that your letter will almost certainly go through the hands of four or five people before it gets to the recipient, if ever. Try to avoid sounding too intimate since this would clearly be inappropriate. Again, sincerity is the key, although, on this occasion, sincerity should be tempered with articulate and positive criticism. Just bear in mind that, although you may know this person's work by heart, you are a complete stranger to them. They may be excited to get fan mail, but they won't be if they think it's from a weirdo.

As a general rule, the more specific you can be about why you like this person's work, the better. Try to concentrate on what you like about the work itself, and not get confused with the person who wrote the book or acted in the film. Think about why you want to write to them.

Dear Mr Bryant,

Last night I finished reading your novel Barrel of Laughs. I really loved it.

It held many personal resonances for me, since I, too, grew up in East Grinstead in the 1970s. I absolutely recognised the streets you describe and I can still savour the rancid taste of that revolting imitation cider from the strange little shop behind the station. A few years ago, I heard that the owner eventually sold up and moved to Devon, where he now runs a small but ineffectual garage.

Anyway, for two weeks of my life I was transported back to the East Grinstead of my childhood and, strangely, I absolutely loved it – which was not at all true at the time.

Looking forward to your next work.

Yours sincerely,

Garth Blakely

GENERAL FRIENDSHIP & THANK YOU LETTERS

FRIENDSHIP

Language and tone both play an important role in creating the right style but the information itself is the most important part of a letter to a friend. Good friends won't want to feel that you are so hung up with grammar that you cannot express yourself freely to them.

Try to be as spontaneous and heartfelt as possible. Liven up the letter by using lots of adjectives and adverbs. Bear in mind that your friends will want to hear not just about what you have done lately but what you *feel* about what you have done. There's not much point writing if the recipient is no clearer about what's going on in your life after he has read the letter than he was before he opened it.

This letter from a painter to a friend is both informative and personal. Its tone demonstrates affection for both the recipient and the subject of the portrait. It is also apparently truthful and sincere and, by revealing some of the thought that goes into her portrait-painting, makes the reader feel that she knows the writer a little bit better than she did before – and also puts her in a special privileged position while feeling simultaneously better informed.

Dear Saskia,

Thank you for your letter. I would be delighted were Heloise to sit for me and if she likes the drawing she is most welcome to have it. Nigel, Lucia's eldest son, has been posing for me for a work in watercolours which came off rather well. Taylor Junior, much as I find his company terrific, is still a remarkably young, young man and could not be expected to accept my point of view about anything, although he is intelligent enough to realise that my ideas may differ from his own.

Painting Lucia is becoming quite addictive. She is so famous now and so naturally attracted towards the images of Lucia Taylor that other people have become used to seeing on screen over the decades. She is 53 and a rich, flamboyant and wicked personality (while still, of course, always the Grande Dame). It is hard to see in her any resemblance to the youthful Lucia with golden curls and a party gown. In my opinion she is far more interesting as she is now, but my star-struck vision might seem harsh and unemotional to those in whom current visual contact is supplanted by amorphous and nostalgic memories.

It is difficult for the public to understand that I am not merely playing the role of an unkind and age-conscious camera but, on the contrary, that I am deeply sympathetic to the mature appeals of my subject.

The countryside is very pretty. I try to go for a ramble on the hills each evening. Lucia and I sit up till all hours gossiping. She is a charming raconteuse and that has come as a delightful surprise.

*I hope to see you before September rolls around and then I will be able to
tell you in person about the Divine Lucia.*

Ruby

This letter from the subject of the above portrait, Lucia Taylor, to a
friend of hers about the painting of Ruby's work, throws a slightly
different light onto the same experience and shows that we can all
be equally sincere while seeing quite different things.

Darling Bobby,

*The children have arrived and amuse us greatly. Ally has chilled us with her
first act of rebellion. We could not locate her diminutive figure at tea-time
whereupon Francesco, quite the traitor, informed us, with an elder brother's
contempt, that 'Ally has gone for a picnic'. Meanwhile, a certain Mrs Burly,
who runs the local (and rather ill-maintained) shop, had located our precious
bundle. Excited by her unexpected brush with celebrity, she asked our darling
to lunch while failing to inform us of this rather bizarre act of unwanted
generosity. Ally insisted on eating her own food – 3 Jaffa cakes and a packet of
Smarties. We swiftly prised our gorgeousness from Mrs Burly's grasping hands
with a promise of organic ice-cream. Francesco, meanwhile, has been given a
three-quarters violin and is taking lessons from a local enthusiast, who is not
always appalling to listen to. Ally and Francesco squabble constantly about the
essential qualities of the term 'music' and, fairly regularly, come to blows.
What a lot Nigel is missing by leaving early for nothing but a supporting role
as a minor but absurdly violent criminal in a Hollywood blockbuster!*

*If nothing occurs to change our plans we shall stay here till well on in
October. Ruby, the artist character from London, says she wants 'to paint
a serious portrait' of me, and should this be the case, we may have to
leave rather sooner. I hope not for I am really rather enjoying it here,
despite the apparent, and absolute, tedium. I enjoy my life when it is not
interrupted by too many days of press intrusion, but those days are
infrequent. I am trying to practise my yoga each morning before breakfast
and then attempt to meditate at 4pm each afternoon for half an hour.
When the sun shines, we sit in it – Gregory and the children down by the
pool and I on my terrace as naked as a peeled potato.*

I read Dickens constantly and Gregory reads out ludicrous highlights from each week's edition of 'Hello' magazine. I read to the children each evening before bed. O how intolerable that ghastly 'Harry Potter' is and yet they do insist on finding it clever. I generally have a restorative nap before dinner, pondering over life's mysteries and some of my Oscar triumphs. I have read the children extracts from Variety and keep a cuttings book handy should anyone express an interest.

Yours affectionately
Lucia Taylor

EXERCISE

1 What do you notice about the landscape from letter 1 and letter 2?

2 Who do you think is more at ease in their surroundings?

3 Whose letter is more personal?

There are no correct answers. The questions are merely designed to draw attention to the slightly differing tones and styles in two letters describing the same time span in the same place.

THANK YOU LETTERS

When someone has given you a present or done you a personal favour, a brief letter of thanks is an appropriate response. A short but appreciative note will do the trick and show that you care.

THANKS FOR HELP

Dear Mrs Brown,

Thank you so much for your assistance in obtaining the library card. I am now getting on with the book as fast as I can and will make sure to send you a copy once it is published.

Yours sincerely,
Anna Smith

It is certainly a good idea to send a thank-you note after you have enjoyed a party or a meal at someone else's expense. At best, people really appreciate this and, at worst, they will take it very badly if you do not.

Try to be brief but with an added personal touch – particularly mention the main course, for example, or how much you enjoyed meeting some of the other guests.

FOR HOSPITALITY

> Dear Susan,
>
> Thank you so much for the delicious dinner.
> The haddock was incredible. I hope the stain came out
> of the tablecloth!
>
> See you really soon,
>
> Claire

Oscar Wilde wrote a particularly long and personal letter to his former prison governor after being released from Reading Gaol. It is both well and sensitively written. Although, of course, it belongs to a very specific set of circumstances, read it and note how he manages to express both sincere gratitude and honest criticism without in any way creating a negative tone.

> Dear Major Nelson,
>
> I had of course intended to write to you as soon as I had safely reached French soil, to express, however inadequately, my real feelings of what you must let me term, not merely sincere, but affectionate gratitude to you for your kindness and gentleness to me in prison, and for the real care that you took of me at the end, when I was mentally upset and in a state of very terrible nervous excitement. You must not mind my using the word 'gratitude'. I used to think gratitude a burden to carry. Now I know that it is something that makes the heart lighter. The ungrateful man is one who walks slowly with feet and heart of lead. But when one knows the

strange joy of gratitude to God and man the earth becomes lovelier to one, and it is a pleasure to count up, not one's wealth but one's debts, not the little that one possesses, but the much that one owes.

I abstained from writing, however, because I was haunted by the memory of the little children & the wretched half witted lad who was flogged by the Doctor's orders. I could not have kept them out of my letter, and to have mentioned them to you might have put you in a difficult position. In your reply you might have expressed sympathy with my views – I think you would have – and then on the appearance of my public letter you might have felt as if I had, in some almost ungenerous or thoughtless way, procured your private opinion on official things, for use as corroboration.

I longed to speak to you about these things on the evening of my departure, but I felt that in my position as a prisoner it would have been wrong of me to do so, and that it would, or might have put you in a difficult position afterwards, as well as at the time. I only heard of my letter being published by a telegram from Mr Ross, but I hope they have printed it in full, as I tried to express in it my appreciation and admiration of your own humane spirit and affectionate interest in all the prisoners under your charge. I did not wish people to think that any exception had been specially made for me. Such exceptional treatment as I received was by order of the Commissioners. You gave me the same kindness as you gave to everyone. Of course I made more demands, but then I think I had really more needs than others – and I lacked often their cheerful acquiescence –

Of course I side with the prisoners – I was one, and I belong to their class now – I am not a scrap ashamed of having been in prison. I am horribly ashamed of the materialism of the life that brought me there. It was quite unworthy of an artist.

Of Martin, and the subjects of my letter I of course say nothing at all, except that the man who could change the system – if any one man can do so – is yourself. At present I write to ask you to allow me to sign myself, once at any rate in life,

your sincere and grateful friend

Oscar Wilde

Oscar Wilde to Major James Ormond Nelson, governor of Reading Gaol (28 May 1897 – a week after Wilde's release from the prison)

Henry James, on the other hand, writes a more jokey and casual letter to Max Beerbohm to say thank you for his positive comments about James's latest novel. By using this easy, humorous tone, he manages to be both grateful for the enthusiasm and, also, to deflect any sense that he might be boasting. It is a good idea when writing a thank-you note in such circumstances to remain as light and humorous as possible.

My dear Max Beerbohm,

I won't say in acknowledgement of your beautiful letter that it's exactly the sort of letter I like best to receive, because that would sound as if I had data for generalising – which I haven't; and therefore I can only go so far as to say that if it belonged to a class, or weren't a mere remarkable individual, I should rank it with the type supremely gratifying. On its mere lonely independent merits it appeals to me intimately and exquisitely and I can only gather myself in and up, arching and presenting my not inconsiderable back – a back, as who should say, offered for any further stray scratching and patting of that delightful kind. I can bear wounds and fell smitings (so far as I have been ever honoured with such – and indeed life smites us on the whole enough, taking one thing with another) better than expressive gentleness of touch; so you must imagine me for a little while quite prostrate and overcome with the force of your good words. But I shall recover, when they have really sunk in – and then be not only the 'better', but the more nimble and artful and alert by what they will have done for me. You had, and you obeyed, a very generous and humane inspiration; it charms me to think – or rather so authentically to know, that my (I confess) ambitious Muse does work upon you; it really helps me to believe in her the more myself – by which I am very gratefully yours

Henry James

Henry James to Max Beerbohm (1908)

HOLIDAY CORRESPONDENCE

These days, many people have telephones in their hotel rooms, or even take their own mobile phones with them abroad, so the point of holiday correspondence is no longer merely to communicate safe arrival. Everyone knows that you could simply stick a stamp on a postcard and scrawl the words 'wish you were here', so a letter from someone on holiday must signify a greater desire to communicate, not to mention a particularly close relationship to the recipient. Bear all of this in mind when writing your letter. Think about the person to whom you are writing. If you are describing a place that they have visited, try to relate your words to aspects of that place that they will recognise. If they have not been there, try to bring the place to life for them with some native colour, the use of adjectives and possibly even some dialogue. Think about the person to whom you are writing and what would interest them. Obviously, if they are not railway enthusiasts there is little point going into a detailed description of your visit to the local transport museum. Likewise, if they have no children they may not be totally engrossed by a long and charming anecdote about what your three-year-old did with her bucket at the beach.

Bear in mind, also, the vagaries of the postal system. If your letter will take three weeks to get home and you are returning yourself in two days and will see the recipient before they receive the letter, then clearly there is little point making an intimate confession of your exploits abroad. You will be able to tell them in person in three days' time. Equally, if you realise as you begin to write that you don't actually have that much to say, then a simple postcard might be better than a sheet of paper, since a primarily blank sheet of paper tends to look bald.

As with many other forms of writing, the best way to learn is to study other people's engaging and well-written letters and see how they did it. Think about which parts interest you, which parts you would have elaborated upon, which you would have left out and which parts would, today, be considered culturally insensitive.

Dear Brett,

We are returning to Ronda tomorrow. I have done some riding. How is Zadie?

I am feeling really swell – swear to God I haven't drunk anything but beer since I left Madrid. It's a damn fine country. I know that, in your dream world, we'd all live in towering urban landscapes surrounded by rich men wearing Armani suits and talking politics on constantly ringing mobile phones. And your hell would be a peach-coloured bungalow in Harrow full of small people eating white bread and impatiently waiting for a little man on a white moped to arrive breathless with a half-cold pizza.

For me, however, heaven would be a big farmhouse right here with Lucinda and I cosying up in a warm, toasty kitchen and a salmon stream flowing past the window. And we would have two gorgeously appointed apartments in the centre of town: one where I would have my wife and be monogamous and love her to the very end of my days and the other where I would have my pouting lady friend and an eternal supply of the softest, most deluxe toilet paper and no plumbing problems ever. And there would be a fine local bull ring where I could watch beasts die bloody, manful deaths day after day and then clamber on to my faithful steed and ride home with my twin boys to my bull ranch where we would gaily chuck around a rugby ball while the boys tussle their golden locks and I order a dry Martini from a devoted and antique family butler. Sipping my third Bloody Mary of the evening, I would just catch them finishing their first Greek wrestling class and then I would celebrate with a quick buttock-level squeeze of the young senorita offering to fill my rapidly emptied glass with yet another top-quality, hand-shaken cocktail.

Well, anyway, we're going into town early tomorrow morning. Write to me at the Hotel Sevilla, Ronda, Spain.

Or maybe you don't like writing? I love it because it makes me feel useful without having done any work at all.

So toodle pip and love to Zadie from us both,

Yours,
River

POSTCARDS

Sometimes you are too busy to write a letter but some communication is better than none. This is the perfect opportunity to send a postcard. Thank-you notes, birthday greetings or simple 'hellos' can all be perfectly expressed in two sentences and at least the recipient will know that they have not been forgotten. Try to avoid obvious clichés like 'wish you were here', but the sheer limitations of the space available should be self-defining. You have not got much room to write anything but your message, so – write your message, possibly add a joke or one extra sentence, and then post that card. Better a simple message sent then a really well-intentioned long letter still in the head.

EXAMPLE 1

Dear Peter,

I really enjoyed talking to you yesterday. Maybe we could actually go and see Hamlet instead of just talking about it? How about next Thursday?

Bertie

23 Easton Place
Streatham
London
SW23 8PQ

EXAMPLE 2

Dear Katie.

Thank you so much for the delicious dinner. Your food is lovely, your house is lovely, you are lovely. Can we meet up again soon?

Steve

23 Easton Place
Streatham
London
SW23 8PQ

ILLUSTRATION 5   Postcards can be used for more than just holiday greetings

LOVE LETTERS

This is potentially the most rewarding, or most hazardous, of all personal correspondence and one in which it is crucial to remember that the letter is a permanent form of correspondence. Your letter could be the emotive and intimate start to something long-lasting and beautiful, or it could be the evidence that fixes your emotions to a very specific moment in time – and one which may not last. Bear in mind that people keep and treasure letters and that love letters, above all, should never be written in the heat of the moment and then posted without rereading.

> ☞ **Never send a love letter in the heat of the moment – you may say things you regret.**

People can be less guarded when they write to a friend. Even the shyest amongst us can suddenly become as expressive as we would wish when faced with pen and paper – and much more so than with email or telephone, which might still be seen as intrusive or threatening. A love letter can be read at a chosen moment and at leisure. It can also be read over and over again. Despite that, or perhaps because of it, try to avoid being too passionate or too over-the-top when putting down your feelings on paper. You may well say the silliest things to your beloved when the two of you are alone together, but you cannot predict the mood that he or she will be in when they open the letter. If you are simple and sincere, however, it won't matter if the recipient reads the letter on the train.

Try not to agonise over many draft versions – the lack of spontaneity will be very easy to spot. Let your loved one know that you miss him or her, but try to restrain your description of your feelings in their absence. If you do not include other, more general, information of interest to your reader and he or she opens it in a bad mood, it could just be the subject of indifference or even ridicule. And one which, at the very worst, might be shown to other people.

Always try to avoid writing and sending love letters in the heat of the moment – either after a quarrel or as a desperate plea for attention on a depressing, rainy afternoon. This is really self-defeating and will do you no favours, particularly since most people are at their least articulate at these moments. If you cannot help yourself and insist on putting pen to paper in a hysterical, lovelorn mood, keep the letter overnight and reread it in the morning. If it still says exactly what you want to say, then feel free to send it, but you are more likely to chuck it in the bin.

Choose your words very carefully, since your letter may be scrutinised for secret meanings many times. A love letter may be a powerful force for the promotion of your relationship. You may suddenly find that you can say all the things you have felt inhibited from saying in person or on the telephone. Whatever its drawbacks, it is fair to say that a handwritten love letter is still the most expressive, the most potent and the most romantic form of communication. There are countless situations in which you might be writing a love letter, and each requires its own particular shade of detail and feeling. It would be impossible to write sample letters for such a personal form of expression, but there follow a number of historic letters in which different lovers, in a variety of situations, express their own particular desires, feelings and requests.

STRAIGHTFORWARD EXPRESSION OF FEELINGS BEFORE MARRIAGE – NO HURDLES TO OVERCOME

39 ORANGE GROVE, SINGLETON
BARTONWICK, BW2 5TS

Beth Davies
19 Singer Street
Liverpool

22 September 2003

My darling Beth,

I know it sounds daft, and I know I only saw you
yesterday, but I really miss you already.

I try to tell you how much you mean to me when I'm with
you, but, somehow, we're enjoying ourselves so much just
doing things and being together that I never actually get
round to stating the obvious – I love you. I hope that's not
too embarrassing. I know it's a cliché but some clichés
are true – I've never felt like this about anyone before.
We have the best time together and when I'm with you,
everything that happens seems suddenly positive and fun
and marvellous. No one's ever made the world seem like
that to me before. It's made such a difference to my life
knowing you. I think you're wonderful – you're so gorgeous
and clever and funky.

I know this letter is all in a jumble and I may not be
making much sense but, to me, it suddenly all makes
perfect sense and I hope it carries on like this for ever.

Daniel

Oh my dearest Friend! be always so good to me, and I shall make you the best and happiest Wife. When I read in your looks and words that you love me, I feel it in the deepest part of my soul; then I care not one jot for the whole universe beside; but when you fly from my caresses to – smoke tobacco, or speak of me as a new circumstance of your lot, then indeed my 'heart is troubled about many things'.

My mother is not come yet, but is expected this week; the week following must be given to her to take a last look at her Child; and Dearest, God willing, I am your own for ever and ever . . .

I may well return one out of twenty. But indeed, Dear, these kisses on paper are scarce worth keeping. You gave me one on my neck that night you were in such good-humour, and one on my lips on some forgotten occasion, that I would not part with for a hundred thousand paper ones. Perhaps some day or other I shall get none of either sort . . . My Aunt tells me, she could live for ever with me, without quarrelling – I am so reasonable and equal in my humour. There is something to gladden your heart withal! So you perceive, my good Sir, the fault will be wholly your own, if we do not get on most harmoniously together . . . But I must stop. And this is my last Letter. What a thought! How terrible and yet full of bliss. You will love me for ever, will you not, my own Husband? and I will always be your true and affectionate

Jane Welsh

Jane Welsh Carlyle, having agreed to marry Thomas Carlyle after thirty proposals (1826)

AFTER REJECTION FOR BAD BEHAVIOUR, HOPING FOR FORGIVENESS

93 HUMBOLT AVENUE, PEARLHAM,
GLOS GL21 9PU

18 Hayward Crescent
Amblesham
Cheshire
AM4 1DU

22 September 2003

Dear Alfie,

I am so sorry. I know that there's no excuse and that nothing I say can possibly remedy the hurt I must have caused you. I know that I've behaved appallingly and I just don't know why I did. I realise that I was very lucky to meet you. I love you and our relationship was really good. And, if it's up to me, I know that it can be again.

I am determined never to make such a stupid mistake again. I hope you believe me and can see your way to trusting me again. It's a horrible thing I did and, if you don't want to see me any more, part of the misery will come from knowing full well that I brought it upon myself. I don't think I've ever felt so miserable but I suppose that's because I really love you and I know I've messed things up.

Please forgive me. Please let me come and see you in person, to try, if not to explain, at least to say goodbye properly.

Yours,

Tania

ON HEARING THE NEWS THAT THE BELOVED HAS BECOME ENGAGED TO SOMEONE ELSE

Dear Rupert,

I was really shocked to hear the news of your engagement. I still can't quite believe it. Until yesterday evening, I was under the, clearly false, impression that you were a nice man.

It's quite possible that, in a few months' time, I will be able to think of our relationship dispassionately. At the moment, however, your behaviour seems deceitful, unpleasant and rude.

I thought I was very happy with you and I guess that Samantha is now labouring under the same misapprehension. I look forward to hearing news of your next engagement.

Yours,

Cecily

Most Loved –

As you know well, this breaks my heart.

I couldn't bear to come and see you.

I can only pray God to bless you – and help me.

Yours,

H. H. Asquith, Prime Minister, to Venetia Stanley (1915)

STRAIGHTFORWARD PROPOSITION

93 Humbolt Avenue, Pearlham
Glos GL21 9PU

18 Hayward Crescent
Amblesham
Cheshire
AM4 IDU

22 September 2003

Dear Sula,

Today I thought of you as I was digging in my garden and I vividly recalled our time in Madeira and how knowledgeable you were about all the tropical plants there. It was a pleasure to wander around the island with someone as charmingly informative as yourself. I know we've only been back a few days, but I was planning finally to make that work trip to Leicester next week and wondered whether I might take you out to dinner while I'm there. Maybe you could suggest a good Portuguese restaurant and I could treat us both to some memories of salt cod (well, maybe not!) and two or three of those delicious egg custard tarts.

Since my wife died I've found it very hard to meet new friends and you're the first person with whom I've relaxed for many years. I believe you felt at ease with me, too.

I don't mean to be forward, but do give me a ring and say that's a good idea.

Yours

,Ivor

REJECTION LETTER

Dear John,

I know that simply leaving this letter on the kitchen table must seem like a total cop-out but, in the circumstances, it seemed the least painful way.

Our relationship just isn't working. I don't know when it began to go wrong, but we just don't seem to have that much in common any more. You do your stuff and I do mine and when we're together we don't really know what to talk about. We don't see each other all week and then, after half-an-hour, we start bickering about really pathetic things. It's just as much my fault as it is yours - or rather, none of it is anyone's fault - but we can't just let our lives drift along like this. It seems to me that we haven't been able to talk about the trivial issues because we were both aware of the large, looming one.

I won't patronise you by telling you what a great guy you are. We both know that's not the point. For a long time I thought I would spend the rest of my life with you but I just don't think that's true any more. One of us has to spit it out otherwise we'll both remain in a state of frozen discontent indefinitely. I'm really sorry for both of us that it had to be me.

I'm going to stay at Susie's tonight and I think it's probably best if we don't speak to each other for a while. I know this letter won't surprise you and I know it's for the best, even if it doesn't seem that way now. I don't want to rub salt into the wound, but I do love you.

Lizzie

SENSIBLE RESPONSE BY A WOMAN ON BEING TOLD THAT HER ENGAGEMENT IS UNACCEPTABLE TO HER PARENTS

My dear Sir

I have just received my father's letter. It is precisely such a one as I expected, reasonable and kind; his only objection would be on the score of that necessary evil money. What can we do? I wish I had it, but wishes are vain: we must be wise, and leave off a correspondence that is not calculated to make us think less of each other. We have many painful trials required of us in this life, and we must learn to bear them with resignation. You will still be my friend, and I will be yours; then as such let me advise you to go into Suffolk, you cannot fail to be better there. I have written to papa, though I do not in conscience think that he can retract anything he has said, if so, I had better not write to you any more, at least till I can coin. We should both of us be bad subjects for poverty, should we not? Even painting would go on badly, it could hardly survive in domestic worry.

By a sedulous attention to your profession you will very much help to bestow calm on my mind . . . You will allow others to outstrip you, and then perhaps blame me. Exert yourself while it is yet in your power, the path of duty is alone the path of happiness . . . Believe me, I shall feel a more lasting pleasure in knowing that you are improving your time, than I should do while you were on a stolen march with me round the park. Still I am not heroine enough to say, wish, or mean that we should never meet. I know that to be impossible. But then, let us resolve it shall be but seldom; not as inclination, but as prudence shall dictate. Farewell, dearest John – may every blessing attend you, and in the interest I feel in your welfare, forgive the advice I have given you, who, I am sure are better qualified to admonish me. Resolution is, I think, what we now stand most in need of, to refrain for a time, for our mutual good, from the society of each other.

Mary Bicknell to John Constable, the painter (1811). She eventually married Constable in 1816

POLITE REQUESTS & RUDE LETTERS

REQUESTS

Sometimes, on a delicate matter involving a friend, or when asking a particular favour, it might be more appropriate, and more respectful, to write and ask, rather than simply to telephone. It shows that you have given the matter some considerable thought and that you really appreciate the effort that your friend is making for you.

Dear Brian,

I know how much you want to emigrate to the States and I know how long it has taken you to get a green card and to sort out the job. I really appreciate everything you've gone through to get to this position. However, I really need to speak my mind about something that's bothering me. When I last visited, you told me how much Peter was looking forward to visiting you and the girls in Colorado and how he had always wanted to see the Grand Canyon.

I don't want to be a sneak but, since that visit, your father has telephoned me three times to lay bare his soul about how unhappy he is that you are moving abroad. He knows how much you want to go and he doesn't want to stop you, but, as your godfather, I wanted you to know that he is just putting on a brave face and that he is, in fact, really upset about the whole thing.

I'm not for a minute suggesting that you should feel guilty about going but would it be, in any way, possible to invite Peter for a lengthy stay? I'm sure you've thought of this already but maybe it would help to articulate the idea before you leave. I really don't mean to interfere, but your dad is my oldest, closest friend and I hate to see him upset.

Do ring me if this doesn't make any sense, or just to tell me that I've got the wrong end of the stick.

Affectionately,

Alan

My dear Prime Minister and Illustrious Friend,

I am venturing to trouble you with the mention of a fact of my personal situation, but I shall do so as briefly and considerately as possible. I desire to offer myself for naturalisation in this country, that is, to change my status from that of American citizen to that of British subject. I have assiduously and happily spent here all but forty years, the best years of my life, and I find my wish to testify at this crisis to the force of my attachment and devotion to England, and to the cause for which she is fighting, finally and completely irresistible. It brooks at least no inward denial whatever. I can only testify by laying at her feet my explicit, my material and spiritual allegiance, and throwing into the scale of her fortune my all but imponderable moral weight – 'a poor thing but mine own.' Hence this respectful appeal. It is necessary (as you may know) that for the purpose I speak of four honourable householders should bear witness to their kind acquaintance with me, to my apparent respectability, and to my speaking and writing English with an approach of propriety. What I presume to ask of you is whether you will do me the honour to be the pre-eminent one of that gently guaranteeing group? Edmund Gosse has benevolently consented to join it. The matter will entail on your part, as I understand, no expenditure of attention at all beyond your letting my solicitor wait upon you with a paper for your signature – the affair of a single moment; and the 'going through' of my application will doubtless by proportionately expedited. You will thereby consecrate my choice and deeply touch and gratify yours all faithfully,

Henry James

Henry James to H. H. Asquith (1915)

On a slightly more mundane but rather more everyday note, we all have numerous reasons to request favours from our friends and a letter can sometimes do the trick in difficult situations or where you do not know the recipient of the letter well enough to telephone. Get straight to the point and be polite.

Dear Mrs Jones,

I have heard from Simon Lovidge that you have a really good voice. I am the choirmaster of the Stourbridge Singers and we are really desperate for a soprano for our Christmas concert.

I know that this is short notice and I am sure you are very busy with your own seasonal arrangements, but if you can participate do, please, ring me as soon as possible on 0304 567 8900.

Whether you feel you are able to participate or not, I really appreciate your taking the time to read this letter and reply.

Best wishes,

Andrew Bannister (choirmaster)

RUDE LETTERS

There are times when a formal letter can be of more benefit in a personal situation of complaint than a telephone call or a physical confrontation. A letter might be particularly appropriate where a problem with a neighbour is involved and where unwanted friction might arise quite easily. It is very easy to lose your temper with the people with whom you live in close proximity – just remember that you might have to face them every day for the next ten years. It is always better to go inside, have a cup of tea and remember that these stories have two sides.

☞ **Like love letters, rude letters should never be sent in the heat of the moment.**

Noisy neighbour disputes can quite often be settled with a polite but firmly worded note, as can issues of barking dogs and footballs through windows. Very few people actually want to be a deliberate nuisance. Bear this in mind, try to use temperate language and try not to be plain rude unless it is absolutely necessary. Just remember that if things are that bad, it is always better to get a solicitor to write than yourself. Unless things have really descended to this level, however, try to make your letter as reasonable and as understanding as possible. There's no point making your situation worse than it is already and never write anything in the heat of the moment that you might later regret. Bear in mind that what you want is to resolve the situation and a conciliatory tone may get you a lot further than a rant.

Dear Mr Jones,

I am sorry to be writing to you but I have been increasingly troubled over the past few months by a really loud noise which seems to come from your house at around 2 a.m. every Saturday morning.

I might be wrong, and I really hope I am, but I assume that it is a member of your household who is causing the rumpus and it is really preventing me from sleeping at night. Perhaps you could check it out and get back to me - or simply ask them to stop.

I am regularly losing sleep over this matter and do not wish to have to take it further. The noise must be driving you crazy, too, so I am sure you will be as glad as me to get it sorted out.

Yours,

Daisy Rocket (from Flat 34)

A RATHER BIZARRE SCENARIO WHERE A LITTLE MORE FORCE MIGHT BE CONSIDERED APPROPRIATE

Dear Princess Bibesco,

I am afraid you must stop writing these little love letters to my husband while he and I live together. It is one of the things which is not done in our world.

You are very young. Won't you ask your husband to explain to you the impossibility of such a situation.

Please do not make me have to write to you again. I do not like scolding people and I simply hate having to teach them manners.

Yours sincerely

Katherine Mansfield

Katherine Mansfield to Princess Bibesco (1921)

5

BUSINESS

LETTERS

- PRESENTATION
- JUNK MAIL
- SAMPLE BUSINESS LETTERS

The content and construction of business letters are, and should be, quite different from personal correspondence. The variety of letters that have to be written every day for business purposes is, of course, endless, but the biggest difference between social and professional correspondence will be tone. Even if you know the recipient of a business letter personally, you should still aim to be as informative and objective as possible. All business letters should be typewritten and the tone should be formal. Bear in mind that a business letter may be passed around from one department to another, may even be read out at a meeting and is, in brief, public property.

You should therefore ensure, even more assiduously than in a personal letter, that what you say is accurate, brief and to the point. Do not exaggerate. Try not to embellish in order to make your point more forcibly – if you have a strong argument, it will speak for itself. Always remember to keep a copy of what you have written – obviously, if you have composed your letter on a computer it will be on the hard disk, but remember to photocopy any other letters.

Do not include any personal comments. It is generally inapprop-riate to add remarks like 'and I really hope Ricky does well in his A-Levels' as a final, throw-away comment. You may think it adds a necessary human touch, but, actually, it just looks unprofessional. Firstly, such comments are totally irrelevant and, secondly, the recipient, or more embarrassingly the recipient's colleague at the next desk, may think that you are trying to pull nepotistic strings.

Bear in mind the following points:

- Think about why you are writing.

- Never start writing until you know all the facts – be well informed.

- Think about the recipient and what's in it for them.

- Compose a rough draft first.

✔ **DO use language that matches the recipient's language level – if you're writing about a business matter to someone who doesn't speak fluent English, keep your language particularly straightforward.**

✔ **DO be as precise and simple as possible – don't waste space.**

✔ **DO double-check your letter before you send it – it's really easy not to spot a mistake first time round.**

PRESENTATION

Business letters should always be easily read and understood. Typing looks more professional than handwriting, though handwriting is not necessarily a disaster. It is imperative that you include your address,

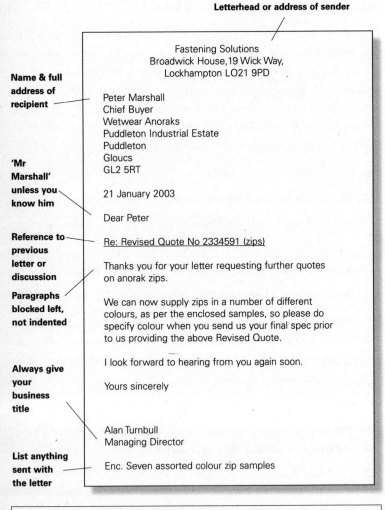

Letterhead or address of sender

Fastening Solutions
Broadwick House, 19 Wick Way,
Lockhampton LO21 9PD

Name & full address of recipient

Peter Marshall
Chief Buyer
Wetwear Anoraks
Puddleton Industrial Estate
Puddleton
Gloucs
GL2 5RT

'Mr Marshall' unless you know him

21 January 2003

Dear Peter

Reference to previous letter or discussion

Re: Revised Quote No 2334591 (zips)

Thanks you for your letter requesting further quotes on anorak zips.

Paragraphs blocked left, not indented

We can now supply zips in a number of different colours, as per the enclosed samples, so please do specify colour when you send us your final spec prior to us providing the above Revised Quote.

I look forward to hearing from you again soon.

Yours sincerely

Always give your business title

Alan Turnbull
Managing Director

List anything sent with the letter

Enc. Seven assorted colour zip samples

ILLUSTRATION 6   Basic elements of a typical business letter the recipient's address and the date: you will almost certainly want a reply and you want to make it as easy for the recipient to respond as possible.

The paragraphs of a business letter are left-blocked, i.e. they are not indented. Leave an extra line of space between each paragraph to make it clearer to read.

If you are writing to a large corporation or company, it is always better to address your letter to a specific person. If you do not know that person's name, ring the switchboard and ask the receptionist for the name of someone within the department you are trying to contact. It is always better to write to a named person.

If you are writing a letter of more than one page, you should always start each page on a fresh sheet of paper. It may not seem eco-friendly, but no one will ever turn over the paper to read the back side of the page. There is no need to number the first page as this will be self-evident from the header on your paper. If you do not have printed continuation paper, however, the top of each subsequent page should be set out thus:

Susie Splinters – 2 – Rosie Alliance

If the pages become lost or separated, everything will then be a lot clearer to your recipient than otherwise. It would be sensible to staple the pages together, in any event.

JUNK MAIL

Letters that are designed to sell a product have common factors and may all, without exception, be classified as 'junk mail'. There are some basic guidelines you can follow in order to avoid your letter being thrown into the rubbish bin before it has even been opened and perused.

✗   **DON'T claim that your product will turn all grey hair blond within minutes: if this is not true, it will not happen and will put people off buying any of your products ever again.**

✘   DON'T use the word 'guarantee' except on very specific, legitimate occasions.

✔   DO be as straightforward as possible.

✔   DO try to revise the appearance and design of your junk mail as often as possible.

✔   DO send material as soon as it becomes available and keep it up-to-date.

✔   DO enclose 'Freepost' reply envelopes wherever possible.

✔   DO try to be as specifically targeted as possible: use your common sense. If you are selling hearing aids, try to target people over fifty, for example.

Compose a simple and straightforward letter: just state, without waffle, what makes your product different from, and better than, any similar goods on the market. A 'limited period only' offer quite often works as an effective inducement to purchase.

SAMPLE BUSINESS LETTERS

BANKS

There is a certain amount of key information that must be included when writing to your bank. Quote the account number clearly at the top of the page, as well as any other relevant information needed to access your details as quickly as possible.

☞ Always put down as much factual information as you can muster. If you don't, the bank will write back to you, requesting further details, and this will only slow matters down.

Mr B. Apple
Bootles Bank
15 Turnover Street
Leeds L7 4SE

12 August 2003

Dear Mr Apple,

Re: a/c no: 657849321

Further to our telephone conversation earlier today, I am writing to
request that a standing order of £34, in the name of
'The Portland Insurance Company', which comes out of the above
account on the 13th of every month, be cancelled.

I look forward to receiving written confirmation from you that this has
been done.

Yours sincerely,

Generally speaking, when dealing with amounts, you should spell out
numbers up to 'ten' and after that you should use figures. There are
numerous other reasons why you might be writing to your bank,
including some of the following common examples:

Mr B. Apple
Bootles Bank
15 Turnover Street
Leeds L7 4SE

12 August 2003

Dear Mrs Jones,

Re: higher rate interest a/c no: 4659900

This morning I received the quarterly statement for the above account.

You will see from the enclosed copy of this statement that, on 3 November, £43.00 was debited from my account under the description 'Direct Debit'. I did not and have never authorised such a direct debit.

I trust that you will rectify this mistake as soon as possible and that my account will be credited with the missing £43. I hope that this error will not occur again.

Yours sincerely,

Dear Mr Burton,

Re. a/c no: 5433216

You may be aware that last month my current account dipped just below the agreed overdraft limit of £500 by under £10. Although I put the necessary money into my account to take it back above this figure within a matter of days, I was still charged the standard £25 fee for this error.

I have been a valued customer of your bank for over eight years and also hold several higher interest accounts at your branch, as well as a mortgage and a contents insurance policy. I have never made such an unfortunate error before and I trust you will agree that, given the circumstances, this fee seems a little harsh.

Could you please, therefore, consider recrediting my account with the £25 and I will make sure, for my part, that this unfortunate oversight does not happen again.

Yours sincerely,

BILLS

OVERDUE BILLS – REQUEST FOR PAYMENT Although you may strongly suspect that the payer is withholding money deliberately, you should always initially treat an unpaid bill as an unfortunate oversight. There is no point doing otherwise – the money may yet show up and you do not wish to ruin a working relationship unnecessarily. Try to tread that delicate balance between getting paid as soon as possible and maintaining good relations.

The first paragraph should be a straightforward reminder of the overdue amount. The second paragraph should always be a pre-emptive strike – just in case the payer's cheque is in the post as you write, remember to acknowledge this possibility. Try to turn the letter into a positive rather than a negative experience, by thanking the payer ahead of receipt, rather than chastising them before it.

The last paragraph should always, somehow, open the way for a payer with difficulties to tell you this. Invite them to discuss matters with you, in a friendly way. If they are really experiencing financial difficulties, they may then feel more able to make you an offer rather than simply hiding, in which case you will not receive any money at all and may be forced to take expensive legal action.

Dear Mr Blake,

Invoice no. 123/99

I write to inform you that I do not yet appear to have received your payment of £650.00 for invoice no. 123/99, dated 13 May. This is now two months overdue and I would be grateful if you could give the matter your prompt attention.

If payment has been made in the past few days, please ignore this letter and accept my thanks.

If, on the other hand, you are experiencing any difficulties with your account, please do not hesitate to contact me on 0753 4322110.

Yours sincerely

Peter Piper

Accounts Department

OVERDUE BILLS – APOLOGIES FOR NON-PAYMENT If, on the other hand, you are the unfortunate recipient of this letter and do not have the means to pay, it is worth bearing in mind that it is always better to deal with this sooner rather than later. Anyone owed money would always rather have part payment than no payment at all and most people will accommodate you, if you can only be polite and appear to be doing the best you can, given the circumstances. Face up to things, apologise and explain yourself – though not in too much embarrassing detail. People will generally accept this state of affairs and try to help you.

Dear Mr Piper,

Invoice no. 123/99

Further to your letter of 15 June, I am writing sincerely to apologise for my non-payment of this invoice and to try to clear matters up. As you know from my telephone calls to your office, I was made redundant from my job (with two weeks' notice) eight weeks ago. Unfortunately this was only a matter of days after you had delivered the shelves – with which we are, incidentally, delighted.

I have, fortunately, now managed to get a new job, although we are still trying to get ourselves in financial order after what has been a very trying period in our lives.

I enclose a cheque in the sum of £200 in part payment of this invoice and I hope this will go some way towards making amends. I shall settle the rest of the account as soon as possible and, once again, I am truly sorry for the delay.

Yours sincerely,

John Blake

BUILDERS

When contemplating building work, it is always a good idea to get at least three tenders (or different quotations from separate firms) for this work. This need not be a complicated letter but should include any appropriate architect's drawings and any other information you feel is relevant. Aim to be as straightforward and factual as possible. Bearing in mind that a building firm is almost certain to be run by men, this is one of the very few examples of modern communication where the use of the phrase 'Dear Sirs' might be appropriate.

Dear Sirs,

Re: 73 Farnham Place, Essex

Further to our telephone conversation of 18 November, I am writing to request a quotation for our conservatory. I enclose the architect's drawings nos 1, 2 and 3/00 as well as the relevant planning permission.

Please do not hesitate to contact me if you need any further information or if you need to visit the house. We look forward to hearing from you at your earliest convenience.

Yours faithfully,

If the tender is not suitable, then, clearly, there is no particular need to respond. No one will think you are rude for not having replied to an unsuitable quotation. If you do select a particular quotation, you will also not need to confirm this in writing since a written contract will almost certainly be inevitable and this will override any casual communication.

After the work has been completed, however, it may not be entirely to your satisfaction. If you wish to dispute the quality of work, this is definitely the time to write another brief but formal letter, setting out your complaints clearly and efficiently. Every tedious matter which went wrong in the work now needs to be listed carefully, since you will either be negotiating a discount on the agreed contract price or a legal dispute is about to ensue. There is no need to be rude. If you have a good case, simply state it clearly and it will speak for itself. A straightforward list of everything that went wrong, without added comment, is probably the best way to proceed at this stage.

Dear Sirs,

Re: 73 Farnham Place, Essex

I am writing to express my concern about the construction of the
conservatory at the above address which was undertaken by your firm.

Work was supposed to be completed on this matter on 24 February and
yet, even yesterday, there were still four missing glass panels and
a number of other matters unsatisfactorily completed or not completed
at all. As of yesterday, you had not attempted any work on this job for
some considerable days and yet your employees have still left a large
number of their tools on site, i.e. in the middle of our kitchen, covered
with dirt and wet paint.

You have failed to comply with repeated instructions to complete work
although you have had ample time and information to do so and you
have, on numerous occasions, undertaken to do so. We have been
particularly concerned at your failure to supply or fit the missing glass
panels since this leaves us exposed both to the vagaries of the weather
and to a wide variety of security risks. Although we have pointed this
out to you at some length, you have failed to do anything to remedy the
situation.

We have also been concerned by the sudden absence of a number of
sundry items, all of which were in our kitchen until your builders arrived.
These are:

Item	Replacement cost
3 CDs	£45.00
Bottle of vintage wine	£23.00
Glass vase	£47.50

In the absence of any other evidence to the contrary, we shall assume
that this is your responsibility and shall deduct the cost of these missing
items from the final invoice.

In the meantime, your builders' communications with us over the last
few days have given us renewed cause for concern both over their grasp
of detail and your ability ever to complete the work to our satisfaction.

You could have finished this work three weeks ago. It seems
increasingly unlikely that you will ever finish it, let alone finish it to our

satisfaction. I sincerely hope that matters can still be settled to the reasonable satisfaction of both parties but this will require much greater commitment from you. If the work is not completed to our satisfaction within the next seven days, and further to all the above information, we shall terminate this contract and pay you on the fair and reasonable basis that our contract envisages.

Yours faithfully,

CANCELLATIONS

Start by giving the main details of the event to be cancelled and explain, politely but firmly, why this is happening. You do not have to go into too much detail, since you do not want your business colleagues to think that your company has financial, or indeed any other, problems. Provide the most general explanation for the cancellation and leave the rest to the reader's imagination.

Always include an apology and conclude the letter by detailing any necessary information for the return of documents or funds.

Dear Mrs Whitewell,

We regret to inform you that the Safety Locker 2000 conference at Stamford Arena on 12 May has been cancelled.

Although many firms have expressed interest in this conference, we have not, unfortunately, received a sufficient number of confirmed deposits to enable us to continue planning this event.

We are very much hoping to reschedule the conference for later in the year and will certainly keep you posted about any developments on this score. In the meantime, we wish you a happy Easter and are returning your documentation and deposit under separate cover.

Yours sincerely,

CHURCH

The three events about which people are most likely to have dealings with their local, or any other, church are births, marriages and deaths. Particularly if you are not a regular worshipper at the establishment in question, it is probably a good idea to initiate proceedings with a letter. This seems polite and respectful, which can only benefit your cause if the church authorities consider you to be the kind of person who may only turn up to services in their building three times in your life.

Do find out the name of the relevant person to whom you should address your letter. This will make it look as if you have at least made some effort.

Dear Mr Burley,

You may be aware that I have become engaged to Miss Eleanor Bowery, who is a resident of your parish although not one of your regular worshippers.

She has asked me to write to you because it would really mean a lot to her to be married in church despite the fact that she feels embarrassed about her lack of attendance there. I know that we have both had periods in our lives when we have lacked faith but, given our new-found happiness, it would mean a lot to both my future wife and myself if you feel that you could accommodate us in your church.

Perhaps we could both arrange to come and see you in the very near future. Please do not hesitate to call me, either at home or at work, if you have any further questions or if you merely wish to have a preliminary discussion.

Yours sincerely,

Dear Mr Burley,

Our son, Edward, was born on 16 February. Although we are not regular worshippers at your church and we appreciate how busy you must be, we are very anxious that Edward should be christened in the church in which both my wife and my wife's mother were baptised.

Perhaps we could telephone you, at your own convenience, in order to sort this out. We were thinking, ideally, of a date in April but we are completely flexible.

Thank you very much for your attention.

Yours sincerely,

COMPLAINTS

It is always a hassle complaining about faulty or unsatisfactory purchases or services. You must obviously write a letter since a telephone call will get you nowhere, but if you are too conciliatory the letter will not be effective. If you are too aggressive, however, you will merely alienate people and you may have to deal with the same firm again in the future. It is also self-defeating to be too rude since you will almost certainly want your money back as quickly as possible and it is therefore in your interests to get the customer relations manager on your side. A fair but firm tone is most likely to achieve the desired result.

Start by stating where and when you purchased the goods in question and then move on to explain why they are not satisfactory. Do not be unnecessarily emotive. Do not be rude. Simply state what the problem is and let the facts speak for themselves.

Provide a full and detailed list of the problems you have encountered and supply a log of any previous communications you have had with the firm about the matter. Wherever possible, state the name of anyone you have dealt with at the firm alongside details of when you spoke to them and what was said. If possible, support your claim with outside expert evidence or independent sources.

State what you wish to be done about the situation – whether you wish for a replacement item or you money back. Try not to be too negative. Try to compliment the firm on whatever aspects of their service you consider to have been satisfactory. Avoid threatening comments but do not rule out the threat of legal action. Be prepared to carry this through, if necessary.

A complaining letter should be a real balancing act. You have to point out what has gone wrong, but you want the recipient of the letter on your side in order to help get it sorted out. You may feel furious at the way you have been treated, but you needn't go in hard in the first instance. If the situation is not resolved quickly, you can adopt a stronger tone in a later letter. Don't fire off all your ammunition in one broadside.

Dear Mr Pettigrew,

Account no. 7645

On 17 February, we purchased a Bryant 754 washing-machine from your store. Since that date it has flooded once and broken down with clothes inside it twice. We have been forced to call out your service engineer on four separate occasions, namely 20, 23, 24 and 28 February. There appeared to be a variety of different problems to resolve – all of which you will see from the enclosed copies of the service engineer's reports.

As a consequence of the above problems, we now have water marks all over our bathroom floor as well as a number of ruined items of clothing. We enclose photographs and a dry cleaner's report.

We have suffered considerable inconvenience and some financial loss since the purchase of this faulty product from you. In the circumstances we must ask you to replace this item within the next seven days and to recompense us for the additional losses we have suffered.

We await your prompt response.

Yours sincerely,

Dear Ms O'Mulligan,

Client ID: 456789

Although we have been in fairly constant communication about the above matter for over a week now, I am now writing this letter to confirm the long and tedious sequence of events which led to my decision today to return the above Crossroads product.

On 10 January 2000, I purchased a Crossroads computer from your shop in Broadstairs Street. Since there were none in stock in your store on that day, I was told that the computer would be delivered to my home address on 12 January. At 9 a.m. on that day, I rang the store and was told that the machine would arrive between 9 a.m. and 5.30 p.m. It did not. At 5.30 p.m., I rang again and I was promised delivery the next day.

On 13 January, having rung your store repeatedly, I was again assured that the computer would arrive that day at any time before 5.30 p.m. Again no parcel arrived. When I eventually rang at 5.30 p.m., I was assured by Mervin Brians that the parcel would arrive by 12 p.m. the next morning without fail.

On 14 January, no parcel arrived and no one rang to apologise. At noon, I rang Crossroads head office and was told that none of these models was in stock and that the computer could not, therefore, arrive that day. Bizarrely, just as I had given up, your van finally arrived at 1 p.m. and delivered two parcels. Having unpacked these, I immediately discovered that the keyboard, the mouse and the software were all missing. I rang again and was told that the third parcel containing these items would be delivered, without fail, the next day. It was not.

It is now 17 January and the missing parcel has still not arrived. Although I have spoken to your customer relations department repeatedly, no one has offered to compensate me for the loss of my time, let alone my telephone bill.

I bought a Crossroads product because so many people had assured me that your service is excellent. It seems they were mistaken. I am now returning what components I have of your product and trust that my Visa account will be recredited with the £799.00 without delay.

Yours sincerely,

Dr Holliday
Dr Chang's Allergy Clinic
Munster House
Harley St
London W1   18 April 2003

Dear Dr Holliday,

I wish that I were writing to tell you how much my skin condition had improved since my appointment with you on 3 April, but sadly the marking has changed very little, despite regular applications of the creams you prescribed. I shall presumably have to search elsewhere for the cure, but one thing still troubles me. You said that, since I had stopped consuming dairy produce, the allergy test conducted by your clinic could not detect whether an allergy was present or not. Does this not invalidate the whole process?

In the meantime, little has changed since before I saw you, except that you are £80 up, whilst I am £102.95 (including the cost of the prescription) down. I wondered if you had any practical suggestions.

Yours sincerely,

Dear Mr Tynan,

Re: 44 Brandon Street, E17

I acknowledge receipt of your letter and invoice dated 10 August 2003.

Having considered your invoice, we consider it to be totally unreasonable for the services rendered. We are sorry that you did not make your fee rates totally clear to us when we hired you and, having consulted a variety of local firms, we consider that £60 per hour (and not the £75 you appear to be charging) is the current acceptable rate for this type of work.

Subtracting the $1\frac{1}{2}$ hours for the abortive meeting with Mrs Brandon which we had previously cancelled, this would make your invoice: 9 3/4 hours @ £60 = £585 plus £34 travel expenses, making £619. With VAT, this comes to £727.32.

We enclose a cheque for this amount, although we stress that this is still far more than we were told the work would cost. Could you please send us a receipt?

Yours sincerely,

Customer Service Department
Holiday Cars

Dear Customer services department,

Re: Booking ref. 345678

From the 11 to 17 June 2003 we hired an Opal Corsa 3-door car through your agency. We picked the car up and returned it to Malaga airport. We paid £79 for the week's hire and were quite specifically told by you that this was an all-inclusive price with no hidden extras.

On arrival at Malaga airport, Holiday Cars informed us that they had filled the car up with a full tank of petrol. We were immediately charged for this petrol as well as deposit money for the car. These figures came to a grand total of 156 euros (£93.65) which was more than we had paid for the week's car hire. I was told that around £30 of this money was for the petrol. On 17 June we returned the car in perfect order and my card was 'fully' refunded although this 'full' refund was only 94 euros.

On 20 August I received my Visa bill, including the figure of £93.65 but not including any of the refund. I must now pay this full amount or I will be charged interest. This is clearly an unsatisfactory state of affairs.

I was never told that I would be charged for a full tank of petrol.

I should not have been charged an excessive amount for a full tank of petrol.

Since I was charged for a full tank of petrol, I should have been refunded for the petrol left in the tank at the end of the trip.

I should not have had the deposit money immediately deducted from my account on 11 June.

Since I was charged the deposit money, I should have been refunded the deposit money, immediately upon returning the car.

I trust that you will deal with all of these points as swiftly as possible and that I will not be left even more out of pocket than I am already.

Yours sincerely,

COMPLIMENT SLIPS

Compliment slips are only really appropriate when the recipient of the mail is expecting some printed information from you and you want them to know it is definitely from you. If you need to write more on the slip than a simple 'Here's the info, Susie'-type message, then you should revert to a postcard or a letter. Compliment slips are invariably handwritten, although, of course, the slip itself is, by definition, printed and designed to look smart and effective.

HOLIDAY ARRANGEMENTS

Travel and holiday arrangements are frequently organised by telephone but, almost invariably, the hotel will insist that you write a letter to confirm your booking and that you supply some kind of deposit with the letter.

> ☞ Holiday details are always best confirmed by letter, even if
> the person you are dealing with does not speak English.

This letter should include a number of important details. You should make sure that you supply them in full and then rigorously check each detail before you post your letter. It is very easy to get confused about dates. Bear in mind particularly that if you are flying from the UK eastbound on a long-distance journey then it is highly likely that you will arrive at your destination the following day. This may sound obvious, but do check. On a similar note, even if your last night in a particular hotel is 12 May, remember that this means you will be checking out on the 13th. Again this sounds self-evident, but it is one of the most common errors when booking accommodation.

Naturally, language may be an issue with this kind of letter. If you do not speak the language, then written confirmation will probably suffice since someone in the hotel will invariably be able to translate your letter. As a general guideline, it is much better to be totally clear in English than to be incomprehensible in Italian.

Whether writing to enquire about or to confirm accommodation, you should always remember to include the following details:

- number of rooms required
- bath, shower or w.c. in the room?
- date of arrival
- date of departure
- is breakfast (or any other meal) included in the price?
- confirmation of price
- particular view requested?
- any other specific requests – children's facilities, etc.

The Manager
Hotel Alvarez Quintero
c/Alvarez Quintero 12
09765 Sevilla
Spain   25 May 2003

Dear Manager,

I found the name of your hotel in the Rough Guide to Spain, where it was highly recommended for the splendid breakfasts.

We are arriving in Sevilla on 14 June 2003 and intend to stay for four nights – that is, until 18 June. If possible, we would like to reserve a room in your hotel for this entire period. We have a two-year-old son, so we would need a double bedroom with an extra single bed. Is this possible?

I understand from the Rough Guide that this would cost around 65 euros a night with breakfast. Could you please let me know whether you have a room available and, if so, please advise me of the total price, including breakfast. If you have any extra information about events in Sevilla in June then we would be very interested to receive this also.

Thanking you in advance,

Alan and Betty Roberts

You should get a response fairly promptly and, once you do, you will need to write again in order to confirm the booking. Many hotels will simply ask you to fax back their letter of confirmation with your Visa card number added at the bottom. In any event, your letter of confirmation should look something like this:

Dear Señor Ramon,

14–18 June 2003

This is to confirm our reservation at your hotel for the above nights. We will require a double room with an extra single bed for all four nights inclusive. The all-inclusive price for the four nights, including breakfast, will be 260 euros.

We look forward to meeting you next month and, in the meantime, I enclose my credit card details, as requested.

Visa No: 4929 5678 1234 0000

Val: 00/01 Exp: 02/04

Yours sincerely,

Betty Roberts

You may, however, have difficulties with your reservation. If you have any queries at all, particularly about the price, then this is the time to resolve them. State the problem clearly, particularly if you are writing to a foreign country. There is no point thinking that you will work it out when you get there – this may well cast a blight on your entire holiday. If you are not entirely satisfied with the response so far, then you should not yet include your credit card details. This will only add to the confusion.

Dear Señor Ramon,

14–18 June 2003

Thank you for your letter of 1 June 2003 in reply to my enquiry of
25 May requesting a double bedroom for the above nights with an extra
single bed for our son.

I note from your reply that you have quoted a price of 65 euros per night
for my husband and me and then an extra 50 per night for my son.
Perhaps there has been some confusion. We do not require an extra
room for my son, who is only two years old, merely an extra single bed
in our bedroom.

Before sending you my credit card details to confirm this
accommodation, I would be grateful if you could verify this arrangement
and that the price of 65 euros a night including breakfast covers all three
of us.

Yours sincerely,

Betty Roberts

INSTRUCTIONS

We all have to issue these formal notices quite regularly. It is best to be as formal and concise as possible. Be specific. Issue your instructions without waffling and do not include any unnecessary detail. Provide any references or account numbers clearly as a header so that your information can be accessed as quickly as possible.

FAO Miss G. Michaels

Further Advances Department
Bangles Loan Company
PO Box 555
Nottingham NG3

17 June 2003

Dear Miss Martin,

Re Roll Number: B/3210-99

Further to your forwarding of £1,970.00 to our builders, Griggs Contractors, I am now writing to request that you send them a second cheque in the sum of £2,034.23. Could you please send this amount direct to them at the following address:

Griggs Contractors

Langly New Road, Nottingham, Notts NW5 4HH.

Could you then send me a cheque for £995.77, in order to make up the rest of the total loan of £5,000.

For further clarification, I enclose a copy of the builder's invoice of 14 June 2003 and your letter of 24 May 2003. I would also note, however, that you have still not written to me to confirm what my new monthly payments will be at the fixed rate (TRT098) of 3.8%. Could you please do this as soon as possible?

Yours sincerely,

Mervin Burwell
ABA Insurance Brokers
12a Highland Close
Cardiff CA3 5RT

Dear Mr Burwell,

Re: House Insurance for 33 Abergar Road, Cardiff CA3

I am writing this note to confirm that, as from today, I wish to transfer the Buildings Insurance policy for 33 Abergar Road away from the Royal Alliance in Swansea and into your hands. As a result of this new arrangement, I will receive back 20% of the policy premium as my annual commission from you.

Having received my instructions I trust that you will now proceed with the transfer as soon as possible.

Yours sincerely,

INSURANCE

Making an insurance claim of any sort can be extremely complicated. Before you begin the procedure, you should study your policy carefully in order to establish whether you are even covered for the problem that has arisen. If you have a £50 excess, for example, and it cost £45 to replace your window after it was broken, then there is no point at all in trying to claim. If you have a £50 excess, however, and it cost £75 to replace your window, do consider factors like whether it is worth losing your no claims bonus for the sake of a mere £25.

Assuming that none of the above applies, you will first want to telephone your insurer in order to request a claim form. For many larger firms today, filling in this form is all that is required to set a claim in action. For smaller firms, however, a letter may be more appropriate. Make sure this letter is clear, includes all the relevant details and maintains a firm grip on the facts. There is no need to tell the insurer how much grief the incident has caused you – you will not get extra compensation merely because you are extremely upset.

☞ **Remember to include any additional evidence, photographs or statements that you have gathered. If you do not, you will only be asked to supply them later on anyway.**

Dear Claims Department,

Re: Policy no. 456789

I wish to make a claim under the above policy for damage caused to my cellar following the recent flooding of the River Uckley. On 13 October, the banks of this river overflowed, causing vast amounts of water to rush through our village.

As a result of this flooding, gallons of water poured into our cellar, causing it to fill up to a depth of over two feet. All four walls and the floor of the cellar are still damp, despite the use of heavy-duty pumps by the fire brigade. In addition, the ceiling in one corner of the cellar has collapsed.

We have had inspections done by three local builders and we enclose their estimates for this work. You will see that the cheapest is £2,400 and the most expensive is £3,500. We are inclined, however, to choose the third quotation (£3,000) from E. Gripps & Sons since it seems to be a sensible middle option. We trust that you will reimburse us in full for this work, since it is covered by Clause 3.4 of our policy.

Please let us know as soon as possible if you have any comments, since we are obviously keen to get on with this work as soon as possible.

Thanking you in advance,

Yours sincerely,

MPs

You may wish to write to your Member of Parliament when seriously aggrieved about a local, or even international, issue. This is often a final resort and their postbags always contain a fairly high percentage of letters dealing with complaints that no one else has taken seriously or wished to address.

Most of these letters will be local community grievances of some description and a Member of Parliament is a perfectly valid person to whom to address these complaints. Bear in mind that she or he may receive hundreds of similar communications, and unless your letter is clear, simple and factual, it may go to the bottom of the pile.

If you do not know the name of your local MP, ask at your local library or town hall. They will be able to tell you the correct name, how to locate him or her and how to address your letter. Just remember that MPs are not the same as general complaints bureaux. Do not attempt to write to your MP unless you have tried other, more easily accessible, paths first and these have all failed you.

Dear Eleanor Bromstone,

I have been one of your constituents for over ten years and have never felt the need to write to you before, but such is my concern that I now feel compelled to take this step.

I have just come out of Mowbray Hospital after undergoing minor surgery on my eye. I am a great believer in the NHS and would never, voluntarily, use private health care but, despite this, I must say that I was shocked by the standards of care on my ward – F5.

I have nothing but praise for the staff. The doctors were professional and competent and the nurses were doing their absolute best to maintain standards but, given the resources available to them, this was simply not possible. During the day there were three nurses for 35 patients and at night the ward was even more drastically understaffed. Everyone was trying hard, but the ward is so clearly understaffed that it is not surprising that, over the three-day period I was there:

1 Several elderly patients wet their beds and were left in soiled clothing for long periods of time.

2 One elderly gentleman fell out of bed and could not be comfortably repositioned for half an hour.

3 The telephone rang constantly and was never answered.

4 Empty plates were left beside beds or on trays for hours.

5 The toilets were, quite frequently, dirty.

6 The nurses' regular rounds were constantly interrupted by more urgent affairs, leaving more mundane but equally important care until much later in the day than should have been the case.

Worse still, morale is horribly low in the entire hospital and this feeds through to the patients. I had the impression that all the staff feel overworked and underpaid and, even granted that a hospital is rarely a joyous place to be, the depressing atmosphere at Mowbray makes even a three-day stay extremely depressing.

I do not think that blame for this situation should be laid on the staff. They are doing an enormously hard job as well as they can. I'm sure you, as our local representative, must be able to do something to improve matters. This is a crucial issue – and a vote winner or loser. Surely something can be done?

Yours sincerely,

PARKING AUTHORITIES

This is quite possibly the most frequently written official letter of all. When you get a parking ticket, it will always state the requisite address on it, as well as the name of the person or authority to whom the complaint should be addressed. Remember that parking fines increase if you do not pay them but are frozen from the day your letter of complaint is received until the date it is dealt with.

If you send a cheque, it will be banked until your letter has been dealt with and the money will then be refunded to you if your letter succeeds. The complaints authorities get hundreds of letters every day, so do not expect to get a response immediately. When you do get a request or a response, however, do not ignore it. Try not to be angry or rude: this will not help matters. The name of the person who gave you the ticket will be marked on the ticket itself so there is no need to add this sort of detail. Merely explain what your reason for complaining is and then set it out clearly and briefly. Try not to take receipt of a parking ticket personally.

Controlled Parking – Finance
Sotherby Town Hall
Stimple Road
Stimple DB5 2RT

17 December 2003

Dear Controller,

Re: Parking Notice Number: AB 1376484848

Yesterday (Saturday) I parked outside Smithy's Bookstore, in Malcolm Street, at 3.40 p.m.

As far as I am aware, it is a national rule that one is allowed to park on a single yellow line after 1.30 p.m. on Saturdays. There was no sign in Malcolm Street to suggest that the law had changed or that Malcolm Street had any other legal peculiarities. Quite clearly, many other people were under the same misapprehension since there were cars parked all the way up Malcolm Street on the single yellow line.

I emerged from the bookshop some 20 minutes later only to see the traffic warden writing out a ticket and placing it on my windscreen. She told me that different laws now apply to different areas and that, if I hadn't known this, I should write to you. I am therefore doing so since what she says may well be true but I could not be expected to know this unless the street is signposted to this effect. It seems deeply inequitable to modify local parking regulations without actually informing any of the locals that you have done so.

I am enclosing a cheque for the required £30 in order to show goodwill but I trust that you will not cash it. I feel very strongly about this matter since there was absolutely no way that I could have known that I was parking illegally.

Yours sincerely,

> ☞ **Do not prevaricate when writing to a parking authority – it is incredibly tedious but any delay will only make things worse for you.**

Notice Processing Office

City of Stopham
P.O. Box 7890
Stopham
ST9 0BQ

22 October 2003

Dear Notice Processing Officer,

Re penalty charge notice no.: WE 228 9493 4

Vehicle Registration Number: T576 BLD

I came out of my house this morning to discover that my car, which was parked outside my front door, had received a penalty charge notice. I have a valid resident's parking permit for Zone 4 which was clearly visible through the windscreen and my car is, incidentally, parked in exactly the same spot every day, displaying exactly the same parking permit. I was therefore astonished to see the parking ticket.

I can only explain this apparent short-sightedness on the part of your traffic warden by the fact that the plastic pouch in which my permit is normally displayed had earlier come unstuck from the windscreen and I had therefore left the parking permit prominently displayed on the dashboard instead.

I have now reattached the permit to the windscreen so that there can be no more room for further short-sightedness on the part of your traffic warden. In the meantime, I enclose a copy of my parking permit no: Z76543 valid until 01 Aug 2003 and your various parking notices.

I trust that you will inform your officer that a parking permit does not have to be stuck to the windscreen in order to be 'clearly displayed' and that this type of incident will not, therefore, occur again. It is not only upsetting but also an absolute waste of my time.

Yours sincerely,

POLICE

The police are always asking for the assistance of the public so, if you feel you have a grievance with which it is inappropriate to deal on the telephone since it is not an emergency, it is always a good idea to write. This may be a complaint about a neighbouring property which you feel has become a drug den or a local street which is considered to be particularly dangerous. Try not to sound like a nosy neighbour or a sanctimonious one. If you stick to simple facts and explain why you are writing clearly and concisely, you will come across as a concerned individual who simply wants to make his or her community a slightly better place in which to live.

On a practical note, try to find out the name of the relevant officer and then address the letter correctly. Aim to create the impression of being concerned without being too personal. Try not to name specific people or places if you are not absolutely sure that they are involved in the incident in question.

Dear Inspector Turbot,

I am writing as a father with a child at the new St Andrew's School Annexe at the top of Harty Road. This annexe has been open since September and over sixty children attend there daily.

Many of the children attending, including my son, have to cross Bunyon Road in order to get to the school gates. As I am sure you are aware, since the opening of the new Tesco store on Waterloo Road three weeks ago, there has been a huge increase in the number of heavy lorries speeding along exactly this part of the road in order to make deliveries to the back of the store via the entrance on Bunyon Road – many of these lorries hurtling along at precisely 8.30 just as my son, and many other children, are arriving for school.

Would it be possible to establish a zebra crossing just in front of the school? Or, if not, would it be possible to place a traffic inspector at the junction at that time in the morning in order to supervise this traffic? This would surely be a sensible precaution given the circumstances.

Yours sincerely,

Dear Inspector Turbot,

Re: 57 Haddock Drive

I live at the above address, just beyond the Balti House, and my garden backs on to the garden of 43 Mullet Road.

For the past four weeks there has been a nightly stream of people traipsing into this garden and then openly weighing small piles of a granular, white material on a set of scales. I, and all my neighbours, are then forced to listen to a nightly party attended by a variety of undesirable-looking people, all creating an enormous amount of noise, clanging spoons together and making a thorough nuisance of themselves until 4 a.m. every morning.

I would certainly not write to you if the noise had only occurred once or twice – clearly everyone is entitled to have the odd garden party – but this is really becoming anti-social and, possibly, dangerous. No one should have to put up with this sort of disruption but particularly not the large number of small children living in the street.

I have tried discussing the noise with the people in the garden myself but have met with both verbal and physical abuse. Could you please investigate the matter?

If I can be of any assistance, please do not hesitate to telephone me.

Yours sincerely,

REQUESTS

Sometimes, just as with personal letters, when a delicate matter involving a favour is requested, it is more appropriate to write a letter since this will seem a lot more formal and respectful. It might confirm a casual request over the telephone, which need not have been granted, or it might simply be a more tactful approach to a possibly unwanted request. The letter shows that you have really given the matter some thought and that you appreciate the extra effort that someone else is prepared to exert on your behalf.

Deborah Morgan
Customer Relations
PO Box 1234
Transit Trains
Birmingham CT18 8XY

15 March 2003

Dear Deborah,

Re: Booking Ref 06055176/01

Further to our telephone conversation earlier this morning, I am writing
to you as requested to return the original tickets for our trip on Transit
Trains.

As I explained on the telephone, I am loath to take my two children by
myself on a trip to visit my parents in Manchester this Saturday since
this is the same day as Manchester United are playing Aston Villa in the
FA Cup at Old Trafford. I would really appreciate it, therefore, if you could
exchange the tickets for travel the following weekend (27 March). I fully
appreciate that the original, special-offer ticket was non-exchangeable,
but I had not realised about the football match when I booked the ticket
and I would be really grateful if you could do this.

Thanking you in advance.

Yours,

In general, asking for a favour should be an extremely straightforward
process. Do not muddle the issue with excess information and do not
beat about the bush. If the favour you require is to do with information,
for example, get straight to the point and make it as easy as you can for
the recipient to reply. Supply him or her with as many response
methods as possible and always include a pre-emptive 'thank you'.

Dear Teddy

I'm writing to ask if you could possibly do me a favour.

For this year's annual conference, we would really like to take all our staff on a trip to Bridgend to learn more about new directional skills in the industry. I seem to remember that your company took a similar course last year and that your group was organised (or perhaps simply led?) by an Australian lady whom you all found inspiring.

Are you still in contact with her? If so, do you think that you could possibly let me have a number for her, or even an address. I know that this might seem a bit cheeky, but we would really appreciate your assistance.

Kind regards,
Luke Schreider

One very specific kind of request letter that requires particularly sensitive wording is the letter requesting a financial donation to a good cause. This cause may be of particular personal concern to you and you may, therefore, feel more sensitive than businesslike about the contents of your letter. This personal concern might lead you to employ a more excessive outpouring of heartfelt words and emotions than you would normally consider appropriate. Your sensitivities, however, should never stop you from including as much relevant detail as you possess. On the other hand, you should try to avoid sounding like a medical pamphlet or a sales manual. Remember that you are not trying to pitch for an account or writing a report. You are simply raising money for a cause in which you believe. The most appropriate means of self-expression, in these difficult circumstances, is simply to state the facts and then let these speak for themselves.

On the other hand, you should also not downplay the good that your cause does. You should not try to lighten the tone by cracking jokes, since this might be off-putting to a potential donor. On a practical note, it is always worth emphasising in your letter exactly what you intend to do with all the money you receive. Accountability is an extremely important aspect of modern charity work. Always include precise information about the charity itself, as well as all the necessary financial information, which should be utterly transparent: how and where does one make a donation? Which credit cards do you accept? To whom does one make out the cheque? All of this detail will give your cause greater credibility and, unless it is absolutely clear and transparent, no one will make a donation.

Always finish by stating exactly how the recipient might find out more about your cause. Try to provide them with a telephone number or an email address – any information that makes your cause seem valid and bona fide is bound to help.

Dear Ms Harvey,

You may have heard that Lucy, the daughter of John and Flora Perty, has been diagnosed with leukaemia and, as a firm, we are very keen to do something to help them at a very difficult time.

After much thought, and having consulted the Pertys, we have come up with the idea of raising the much-needed funds to send Lucy, along with her parents and her brother, Mark, to New Mexico to have a course of specialist treatment at the Splotch Foundation. This treatment, which, sadly, is not available at all in the UK, let alone on the NHS, has been remarkably effective on a number of former patients.

We would dearly love to be able to raise the entire £14,000 that the Pertys need to make this trip. We have been told by the Foundation that the particular course of treatment that Lucy requires will cost in the order of £10,000. The extra money is to fund the necessary air fares for all the Pertys as well as their accommodation and other expenses while in the States. As soon as we have reached our target figure of £14,000, we will stop collecting, since the Pertys do not want to receive any surplus money for themselves.

If you wish to make a donation, cheques should be made payable to 'The Lucy Perty Fund' and then forwarded to me at the office. Alternatively you can pay the money in directly to the Royal Bank at 47 High Street, Aldergate. The account number is 34567800.

If you have any further questions or have any good ideas about fund-raising activities, please do not hesitate to contact me.

This is such a good cause for such a deserving family. We really hope you can help.

Many thanks,

Lily Plunkett
Administrator

It would be ideal if you could respond personally to every charitable donor as this will show that you really appreciate what they have given, help to build a sense of solidarity among the donors and increase their goodwill for any future campaigns. People like to feel appreciated and also like to feel that they are at the heart of something good. Use the thank-you letter to keep them up to date with the fund and with any developments that might have occurred. But most of all, use it to say 'thank you'.

Dear Mary,

Thank you so much for your donation of £20 to the Lucy Perty Fund.

So far we have managed to raise a massive £11,500 and we are delighted for the Pertys. We hope to have raised the entire amount by 1 November, so that Lucy can fly to America, complete the course of treatment and still be home to celebrate her 12th birthday on 17 December.

Any further ideas on fund-raising would be great but, in the meantime, many thanks again for your contribution.

Best regards,

Lily Plunkett

SCHOOLS

Most correspondence with schools involves the perceived lack of academic progress of a child by his or her parents. Other issues that might compel you to write could include discipline (or lack of it) at school; an injury in the classroom; or an appeal to a popular school to take your child in as a pupil. Since all of these are highly emotive matters, it is important to follow basic guidelines. Be as honest and direct as you can, while avoiding direct confrontation, and, without ~~being~~ rude, do not try to be unnecessarily diplomatic. Always address ~~it~~ to the head teacher and try to make it as correct as possible.

Dear Mrs Smythson,

My daughter, Elize, has been attending St Edmund's for over two terms now and my husband and I are beginning to be seriously concerned about the progress she is making at your school.

I am by no means a 'hothouse' parent and absolutely do not approve of constant pressure and examination of young children. Her lack of academic progress, though apparent, is not the issue here. More critical for us, however, is the transformation in our daughter's personality over the last two terms. When Elize started in Year One at St Edmund's, she was a friendly, outgoing child who could read fairly fluently and appeared to be articulate, open and well informed.

Over the past two terms, her reading skills have, apparently, deteriorated rapidly and she has become a shy, withdrawn child who does not like to open a book in public. On the rare occasion when we can persuade her to take her packed lunch to school, she comes home with the food untouched.

We can only conclude from the startling changes in her behaviour that she has been the subject of some bullying at school. We have asked her about this as sensitively as we can but she will not, or cannot, articulate her thoughts. We have mentioned it to her form teacher, Mrs Jolly, on several occasions and still the problem has not been addressed.

This is clearly an extremely serious matter. Could you please meet us urgently to discuss what might be done? We are very unhappy about the situation but, and much more importantly, so, clearly, is our six-year-old daughter.

Yours sincerely,

Dear Mrs Trumpington,

My son, Percy, arrived home from school this afternoon with a black eye and a bad graze on his left arm. We were informed in a note from his form teacher, Mr Hoggins, that this was the result of a playground fight between a few boys and that 'boys will be boys'.

We are, of course, grateful that Percy was sent to the school nurse immediately and that she dealt with the matter efficiently. We are, nevertheless, concerned that this sort of incident should be happening within the school grounds at all.

Perhaps more playground supervision by staff is needed. Or perhaps certain, more active, children could be offered extra activities at lunch-time in order to keep them fully challenged. Perhaps we could come in to discuss these issues with you. We would be grateful.

Yours sincerely,

TRANSPORT ISSUES

With the arrival of various passengers' charters, it is always worth complaining if you have endured a delayed or interrupted journey. It will make you feel better and should result in your receiving some compensation. As with general complaints letters, try to be as unemotional and factual as possible.

Customer Relations

West Coast Line
Euston Station
London
NW1 3RT

26 February 2003

Dear Customer Relations Officer,

I am writing to complain about the inconvenience caused to me by the delayed service on the West Coast Line last week.

I had reserved a seat on the 09.25 from Lancaster to London Euston on 20 February which was due to arrive at Euston at 11 a.m. I was then planning to catch the tube to Paddington in order to get another train to Oxford at 11.45. On purchasing the ticket, I was assured that the 09.25 was the appropriate train to catch and that I had nothing to fear. In all good faith, I bought a ticket for this train.

The 09.25 stopped for an hour for no apparent reason somewhere near Luton. No announcements were made about what was happening; nobody went through the train to apologise and no information was forthcoming about when the train might be expected to start moving again. It eventually arrived at Euston at 11.50, meaning that I had missed my next train before I even got off the first one. The result was that I missed a crucial business meeting, was held up on the way home and returned to Euston too late to catch the last train back to Lancaster. I then incurred the added expense of a night in a hotel in Euston.

I am extremely unhappy about this state of affairs. I always choose to travel on the train if I can. I write this letter not merely to claim the compensation to which I know I am entitled but also to say that, unless you can improve your shambolic service record, I shall be taking the plane direct next time I have to make this journey.

I look forward to receiving your response as soon as possible.

Yours sincerely,

6

TECHNICAL

MATTERS

- HEADINGS
- PRESENTATION FACTS
- MEMOS

Letters involving technical information and their consequent reports can be extremely complicated, with little 'real' text. It is important to follow basic guidelines to make them as legible as possible. In any such report there will have been an initial gathering of relevant technical data which may happen over a long period of time; analysis of this data may have taken even longer.

Combining these elements into a report will then be a matter of selecting the appropriate material from all this technical data and collating it into a logical, legible format. Bear in mind that technical reports must be more evenly balanced and argued than various other forms of correspondence. The case in favour of the report's conclusions must be fully justified and the arguments against it fully investigated. A technical report should have the appearance of being an impartial investigation.

The letter should read in a logical sequence, for example:

1 The terms of reference of the investigating team.

2 An outline of the problem.

3 A detailed account of how the problem was handled.

4 General conclusions.

5 The reasons for other possible conclusions having been rejected.

6 The recommendations made.

There are other general guidelines, which should also be followed:

HEADINGS

Technical information may involve a lot of quite boring detail. Try to break this information down into small, manageable paragraphs. Use as many appropriate headings as possible. These could be as simple as: Contents, Introduction, Conclusions, Recommendations, Appendices and Acknowledgements, but they should always be in bold and clearly flagged.

When discussing technical detail, make sure you steer clear of the jargon. This may seem obvious, but phrases or terms that are clear to you might be jargon to someone who is not as familiar with your field as you are. Keep your text as free from this specific jargon as possible. This applies particularly to computer-related matters.

PRESENTING FACTS

This is naturally going to differ wildly, depending on the subject matter of the report, but there are some general guidelines to follow. Try to lay out the facts as clearly as possible. If there is any doubt in the argument, the adverse evidence should be fully investigated, not suppressed.

Establish and explain your purpose

Identify your course of action

Identify problem areas and outline conclusions

Make appropriate recommendations

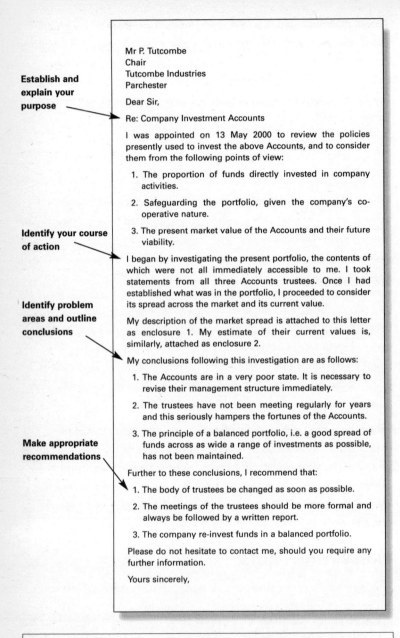

Mr P. Tutcombe
Chair
Tutcombe Industries
Parchester

Dear Sir,

Re: Company Investment Accounts

I was appointed on 13 May 2000 to review the policies presently used to invest the above Accounts, and to consider them from the following points of view:

1. The proportion of funds directly invested in company activities.

2. Safeguarding the portfolio, given the company's co-operative nature.

3. The present market value of the Accounts and their future viability.

I began by investigating the present portfolio, the contents of which were not all immediately accessible to me. I took statements from all three Accounts trustees. Once I had established what was in the portfolio, I proceeded to consider its spread across the market and its current value.

My description of the market spread is attached to this letter as enclosure 1. My estimate of their current values is, similarly, attached as enclosure 2.

My conclusions following this investigation are as follows:

1. The Accounts are in a very poor state. It is necessary to revise their management structure immediately.

2. The trustees have not been meeting regularly for years and this seriously hampers the fortunes of the Accounts.

3. The principle of a balanced portfolio, i.e. a good spread of funds across as wide a range of investments as possible, has not been maintained.

Further to these conclusions, I recommend that:

1. The body of trustees be changed as soon as possible.

2. The meetings of the trustees should be more formal and always be followed by a written report.

3. The company re-invest funds in a balanced portfolio.

Please do not hesitate to contact me, should you require any further information.

Yours sincerely,

ILLUSTRATION 7   Facts should be clearly presented in a business letter

Arrange the information in a logical sequence – if there is any kind of 'story' involved, follow it through chronologically. If there is a daunting amount of data or discussion, it is often helpful to summarise this information at the end of each paragraph. Do not be afraid to use tools like bullet points, or even charts, which can make your letter more easily comprehensible.

MEMOS

Memos are most appropriate for internal communications within a large company when these may need to be recorded for posterity. If you work in a solicitor's office, for example, you may have taken a phone call from another in-house solicitor's angry client and then feel the need to put this conversation down in writing, should the matter ever be taken up against your firm. In other words, the memo is a casual form of recording material, but one that can be used as hard evidence. Email is, quite often, simply the modern form of the memo (see chapter 10).

MEMO

Date: 21 June 2003
From: Eliza Biggins
To: Martin Spicks; Louise Porter, Jed Evans
cc: Holly Fernhead

We have a lot of work to do on the Boston project. Please remember to allow for the 163cm window and not to deduct for wood items.

Thank you.

ILLUSTRATION 8   Typical layout of a short memo

7

EMPLOYMENT

CORRESPONDENCE

- JOB APPLICATIONS

- REFERENCES

- REJECTIONS

- LETTERS OF RESIGNATION

- COMPLIMENTING AN EMPLOYEE

- REPRIMANDS

- DISMISSALS

Letters to potential or current employers or employees may be some of the most delicate you will ever have to write. When you are recruiting potential staff, it is important to create just the right impression since your letter is the sole representative of your firm and the potential employee will be clinging to its contents both for clues and for positive feedback. Rejecting potential staff after an interview is, if anything, a job worth doing with even greater sensitivity – the person you reject today may be absolutely crushed by your decision or, even worse, might be your own boss on a future occasion. Clearly the most critical letters in this category are letters of dismissal – these must be very carefully handled, both because of the feelings of the employee and because of potential legal claims.

Letters to potential employers pose different but equally hazardous problems. A well-written covering letter may not guarantee you a job but a poor letter will certainly ensure that you do not even get an interview – however impressive your qualifications.

Either way round, it goes without saying that this is not an area of letter writing to be dealt with lightly.

JOB APPLICATIONS

Many job applications never even get to the interview stage. Candidates are eliminated from the selection process before this begins because their applications are simply not good enough. An application will normally consist of a CV and a covering letter. It is important to create a well-presented CV, but this section is primarily about the covering letter that accompanies it. Much of the advice is, however, applicable to both parts of the application.

It is a good thing to bear in mind the main reasons for rejection of a job application:

PRESENTATION NOT GOOD ENOUGH Spelling and grammar are poor, while the paper may be tatty and the handwriting illegible.

CONTENT DOES NOT MEET THE REQUIREMENTS If the advertisement asks for current salary, then give it (or state why you have not done so). If photographs are requested, send one and don't attempt to make funny comments about how ridiculous you look in the image – no one will laugh!

IGNORANCE Try to do some basic homework. Find out about the particular company you are applying for and tailor your letter to this information.

LETTER DOES NOT FIT JOB PROFILE If your previous job means that you don't quite fit the job profile requested in the advert, then explain why you are applying anyway. Then go on to describe why you feel that you are the best candidate for the job despite this apparent discrepancy.

DON'T BE OVER-CONFIDENT However confident you may feel that this is the perfect job for you, always bear in mind that you will generally be working with other people and they will want to like you. They will not be disposed to do so if they think you are a boastful show-off.

NEGATIVITY You may feel that the potential employer will almost certainly not want someone who has been abroad for four years or will not want a female in the role, for example, but don't dwell on this. Spend time on all the parts of your application that best fit the job description and write about them in a positive way without being too apologetic or too humble. If *you* don't think you are right for the job, then a potential employer certainly will not. In addition, try to sound genuinely enthusiastic about the job in question.

LETTER FULL OF INCONSISTENCIES You write in your letter that you have been a qualified accountant for the past four years but your CV says that you only qualified three years ago, for example. The potential employer will merely think that you haven't got the necessary eye for detail.

COVERING LETTER

Dear Mr Timothy,

I am replying to your advertisement in the Guardian on 14 June for an in-house accountant.

I am extremely interested in the possibilities that this job holds. Last year I attended the 'Burley House' conference where I listened to your director of finance, Miss Smithy, talking about your policies on tax incentive breaks for professional sportsmen and women. Her material was so positive and so dynamic that it made a deep impression on me and I thought at the time that your company must be a very progressive and exciting place at which to work.

You will see from the enclosed CV that, until now, I have been working in a general employment field but I am particularly interested in the world of sports employment – I attended the conference out of personal interest – and seeing your advertisement has inspired me finally to make that move.

I already have a lot of relevant experience in related fields but I would find the challenge of matching this to your specific requirements one that I would really want to rise to, since it is something I have been contemplating and researching for over a year now. I was merely waiting for the perfect opportunity to come along and it seems to me that your position could be this moment.

I really look forward to discussing the job with you in greater detail. I have a lot of ideas for raising team profiles in this area, particularly in the field of tennis, and I would be delighted to share them with you at the earliest possible opportunity.

I hope to hear from you soon.

Yours sincerely,

REFERENCES

REQUESTING

Requests for references are generally sent out after you have interviewed someone for a job but before you have absolutely decided to employ them. This may be an awkward letter to write since you know that the prospective referee would not have been put forward unless they were likely to promote the candidate's interests. Insist that the referee be someone from the candidate's most recent job and try to ensure that this person was their immediate superior and not a close friend and peer. Try to establish why they left their old job and do not be afraid to ask direct and possibly indiscreet questions. Always give the referee the opportunity to respond by telephone since this may be both more convenient and encourage a greater honesty in response. It also gives you the opportunity to ask further, more searching questions.

Dear Mr Ligati,

Penelope Pit-Stop has applied to us for the job of assistant transport manager, details of which are enclosed. I am writing to you since she has nominated you as one of her referees.

We would be grateful if you could answer the following questions, the answers to which will, of course, be treated in the strictest confidence.

1   How long did Miss Pit-Stop work for your company?

2   Was she a satisfactory employee?

3   Why and when did she leave?

4   Would you re-employ her?

I have enclosed a stamped addressed envelope for your reply but if you would prefer to discuss this matter on the telephone, please do not hesitate to call me on my direct line: 09786 343546768.

Thanking you in advance.

Yours sincerely,

Philip Honda

Director of Personnel

RESPONDING

A reference should generally be a concise summary of the individual concerned. Many larger companies these days merely send out a standard questionnaire with various specific boxes to be filled.

If you are asked to write a reference, you should bear in mind that a personally written letter of this kind is getting rarer and that it therefore requires both total accuracy and brevity. All reference letters should be marked 'Private & Confidential', as should the envelopes in which they are posted.

Writing a reference for an employee whose work has been exemplary is, clearly, not going to be too difficult. Bear in mind the specifics of the job she or he has been offered and then take it from there.

Dear Mr Honda,

Thank you for your letter of 12 June.

Penelope Pit-Stop has been working for our company as deputy assistant transport manager for the last five years. She is a conscientious and dedicated member of our team and her work has always been excellent.

She is now seeking alternative employment because she is getting married and, since her future husband lives in Halifax, she feels it would be unrealistic to commute to Leeds each morning.

We shall be very sorry to lose her but fully understand her reasons for leaving and wish her every success in her future career.

Yours sincerely,
G. Ligati

There is, however, the other side of reference writing – being asked to supply a recommendation for a member of staff who has been difficult, unreliable and less than satisfactory. The best approach to take is to be as general as possible. You should not be rude or derogatory about the candidate as this can get you into all sorts of trouble. Omissions, in any case, speak louder than words.

Dear Mr Honda,

Thank you for your letter of 12 June.

Penelope Pit-Stop has been working for our company as deputy assistant transport manager for the last five years. She has generally been a punctual and pleasant employee and is now leaving, as I understand it, because she wishes to live closer to her future husband.

In answer to your fourth question, I can envisage no situation, at present, in which it would be appropriate to re-employ Miss Pit-Stop since we cannot, in truth, give her the promotion that she feels she deserves. We fully understand her desire to move higher up the career ladder, however, and wish her every success in her future career in the transport industry.

Yours sincerely,
G. Ligati

REJECTIONS

This is, by definition, a tricky area of communication. You will wish to be polite and tactful but you will also wish to discourage the applicant from constantly re-applying to your firm in the hope that they have just managed to get a foot in the door. Always acknowledge the application and refer to the job in question. Move straight on to the rejection itself, remembering to express regret but conveying the information in as bland but firm a style as possible. Make clear that the rejection is final.

Always soften the tone in the final paragraph, wishing the candidate good luck in their future career. There is no point causing any greater disappointment than necessary.

Dear Mr Baldwin,

Thank you for your application for the position of Personal Assistant to Miss Jenkins.

We have considered your letter very seriously and, although we were particularly impressed by your application, we regret to inform you that you have not been successful on this occasion.

We would like to take this opportunity to thank you for your interest in our company and to wish you the very best of luck for your future.

Yours sincerely,

LETTERS OF RESIGNATION

Even if this seems straightforward, always bear in mind the broader issues. If you write a letter of resignation, it will almost certainly be taken at face value, so do not even consider such a step unless you are sure you want to go. If you really are committed to leaving, however, there is every reason to part on good terms with your employer and every incentive to be as tactful as possible. Even if you have already found a new job, your current employer might be a useful referee in the future or you may even return to the company at a later date, far higher up the corporate ladder. Basically, you never know what might happen in the future, so don't burn your boats.

Dear Mrs Porky,

I am sure you are aware that, for some time now, I have been anxious to use my language skills to greater effect. I have been very happy at Pig Purchases over the last two years but I am, by training, a linguist and the export market for your products, with the subsequent travel involved, has, as we all know, not quite developed in the way we had all expected.

I have now found a job with PinkyPerky.com in their foreign licences department and am therefore writing you this letter to give you the requisite one month's notice. I am sorry to leave you, especially at what I know to be a difficult time for the company, but I feel very strongly that this is the right time for me to make this move.

While I wish to join PinkyPerky.com as soon as possible, I would not wish to inconvenience you in any way. If you would like me to stay on for the full month, I shall be very happy to do so. If you could let me know your thoughts on this matter as soon as possible, however, I would be grateful.

Yours sincerely,

COMPLIMENTING AN EMPLOYEE

When an employee has performed a particularly commendable act for your company, a written letter can be a really valuable tool in boosting staff motivation. Not only does it show that you really appreciate the commitment involved, but the member of staff can then show the letter to his or her fellow employees. Without being in any way patronising, this single letter shows that you care about your staff and their performance and may also encourage other members of staff to show the same care in their work.

A handwritten letter might be appropriate here and the message should be totally direct, simple and concise.

> Dear Lucia,
>
> I just wanted to write and thank you for the way in which you dealt with the Italy merger.
>
> This was a very complex, and sometimes tedious, matter which I know took up a lot more of your time than we had all expected. I thought you dealt with it in an extremely dedicated, utterly professional manner and you never lost your temper, even when it looked as if the whole deal might fall through.
>
> We all appreciate how much time you have had to spend away from your baby because of this merger and I hope things will ease off a little for you now. You have done an excellent job. Thank you!
>
> Best wishes,

REPRIMANDS

A written warning should only ever be given once informal discussions have already failed to achieve the desired results. In this context a letter may have serious legal consequences and so should never be issued without due thought. Exercise judgement before you write the letter and make it as fair, accurate and detailed as possible. Do not rely on office gossip. Do not descend to the level of personal insult. Always try to ensure that you are writing a letter without resorting to your own personal bias or prejudice.

Bear in mind that the letter will remain on file and may lead to dismissal in due course. Also bear in mind that it may, eventually, be used as evidence against you at an industrial tribunal. Without being overly dramatic, therefore, set down your warning as carefully and thoughtfully as possible and always allow for any extenuating circumstances.

On a practical note, always set out the specific allegations you are making clearly in the first paragraph, with reference to previous verbal warnings if appropriate. You must be seen to be fair, so always mention any relevant positive aspects of the employee's behaviour. Finally, set out clearly in which ways you would like to see the employee's work improve.

---

14 November

Dear Fred,

On 12 November, I was shocked to learn that the order which you received from Pring & Pring on 29 October had still not been acknowledged by our firm. I was even more horrified to have to learn this news from Mr Pring himself, since Pring & Pring are among our most respected clients and we rely heavily both on their business and their goodwill. As I told you at our meeting this morning, I assured Mr Pring that this kind of incident is very unusual in our firm and that this kind of delay has, to my knowledge, never happened before. I personally guaranteed that the order would be processed within 24 hours. I trust that you will, therefore, deal with this matter without further delay.

I am also unhappy to have to note that your attendance and time-keeping of late have been, to put it mildly, erratic. On 27 October you wandered in to work at 10 a.m., looking rather confused. On 5 and 9 November you didn't appear in the office until around noon and on 13 November you did not show up for work at all.

I have spoken to you several times about this apparent inability to keep time. You have told me twice that you will make every effort to improve your punctuality but, after each assurance, this appears only to have worsened. If you are to continue working for the company, it is absolutely essential both for your self-respect and for our efficiency that your punctuality improves.

I have always thought that Trimble & Gunn was a happy and supportive place to work. If you think that this is not the case, or if you have any specific problems that you wish to discuss, please do not hesitate to make an appointment with me. If not, could you please simply attempt to improve your behaviour or I shall be forced to take further measures myself.

Yours sincerely,

DISMISSALS

Dismissing a member of staff is a very stressful task which should be undertaken with care. If the dismissal is judged to have been made unfairly, you could face legal action resulting in compensation or even reinstatement. Dismissal must, therefore, be treated as a last resort, only to be carried out after all else, including numerous written warnings, has failed. Never write anything that could be considered defamatory. There is no need to be too specific. Unless actual criminal action is being pursued, do not mention dishonesty, however strong the evidence. Try to keep the letter as pleasant and factual as possible. If in doubt, do take legal advice before writing your letter. Be as cautious as possible when dealing with the law. Make notes of everything that is said and done. As soon as it becomes apparent that you are going to have to dismiss someone, start writing down anything relevant that takes place. This may become evidence if you are taken to an industrial tribunal. Never be unnecessarily rude.

Notify the employee of their dismissal and give a termination date in accordance with the relevant legislation or contractual obligations. Clearly but firmly state the reasons for dismissal. Express regret and, if at all possible, offer some kind of compensation package in lieu of notice. Once an employee knows they have been dismissed, there is little point in their attending work.

Dear Mr Partridge,

Following my letter of 14 November and our meeting of 1 December, we are writing to inform you that your employment with Trimble & Gunn will terminate in two weeks' time, on 15 December.

Your dismissal follows numerous verbal warnings as well as the written warning of 14 November. We have given you many opportunities to alter your behaviour but, unfortunately, your attendance and time-keeping have only deteriorated. This week, for example, you have been late on each morning that you have attended, choosing not to do so at all yesterday.

We regret having to take this action but things could not go on in this way. We are sorry that your conduct has left us no alternative.

Yours sincerely,

8

COMMUNICATING WITH

THE MEDIA

- REQUESTING MEDIA COVERAGE
- DECLINING MEDIA COVERAGE
- LETTERS TO THE EDITOR
- PERSONAL LETTER
- SPECIFIC ARTICLES
- GENERAL GRIEVANCE LETTER

Talking or writing to the media might at first seem rather daunting, but it's not something that you need worry about. There are a few basic rules to follow in order to avoid any major pitfalls but, for the most part, using good old common sense will see you through.

REQUESTING MEDIA COVERAGE

It is always worth trying to obtain some press coverage when you are starting a new business, launching a new range of products or simply opening a shop. Always remember that a newspaper is a fast-turnaround product, so unless you are bang up-to-the-minute with your information, you do not stand a hope of getting it in the paper. Don't send the information too early, because it will go into a pile and get lost, but don't send it after the event, since, by then, it has become yesterday's news. Keep the letter short, write it about a week before the intended launch and then fax it through to the newspaper, marked for the attention of a particular person, preferably the editor of the section in which you would like the piece to appear.

Make the letter as short and sexy as possible. Anything glamorous or interesting that you can possibly think of to say about your product should be said now, but in brief. Explain why you think the newspaper's readership will be interested in the project and include all the relevant facts – dates, times and telephone numbers. If it's appropriate, mention that you can supply relevant pictures but also that a newspaper photographer is welcome to attend. Try to include any relevant 'pull quotes' from famous people or other newspapers, endorsing your previous work, and try to make the presentation of your letter stand out – although not in too ridiculous a way. If an editor has fourteen press launches to choose from on a particular day, he or she will need a justifiable reason to select yours. If you are going to take the 'undeniably weird and eye-catching' approach, however, make sure that this is a suitable one for your particular project and try to check that your recipient is the kind of person who might find this funny (or at least newsworthy).

If you feel that your product would be more suited to magazine coverage, then do bear in mind that the contents of most major monthly publications are organised three months ahead of publication date. If your event is in March and you are ringing during the last week of February, the magazine may already be in the shops.

✔ **DO try and follow up your letter with a personal call to a specific person. If an editor likes you, this may make all the difference.**

Dear Miss Jolley,

Margaret's Children

I'd like to invite you as my guest to one of the special advance preview performances of Margaret's Children at Marylebone Station, which are being staged from 8 to 11 February 2003.

It's a really unusual show, not least because it marks the London debut of Toby Popkin, who has been a big star in his home town, Hull, for over ten years. Following the granting of a special licence by Westminster Council, however, this show also marks the first live performances of a theatre play in the concourse of a major London railway station.

Popkin, well known from his roles in Jumping Bunnies and Turnip Fields, is joined on the temporary stage by Eleanor Rabbit, winner of the Best Actress Award at the Newark Film Festival for last year's arthouse hit, October Aliens. She was also the star of Rainbow Georgie, about which reviewer Lila Jenkins wrote: 'absolutely delectable'.

The play itself is both written and directed by Joseph Popkin, Toby's father, who won a Silver Button Award for his work on the geriatric bowling documentary Skittles at Sunset, which was described in Variety as: 'a luminous work, for which much credit must go to the distinctive directorial skills of Popkin'. This is the first time that Toby and Joseph have ever worked together.

All in all, this is a really strong artistic team, while the play itself is a skilfully conceived underworld entertainment concerning the bare-knuckle adventures of the dubious types who hang around the outskirts of urban railway stations. It's comic, confident and cute and Toby's charisma makes him ideal for the part of Stiff, a short but plucky railside risker.

I really hope that you'll be able to make it. It should be a remarkable, and highly entertaining, evening of theatre. Do give me a ring if you'd like to come along.

Best wishes,

Dear Peter,

THE COMEDIAN LEE PARSLEY RETURNS FOR TOUR OF UK

'Parsley held the audience riveted with a succession of deftly delivered one-liners . . . on a comedy circuit awash with competent yet unengaging mediocrity, Parsley's ability to captivate an audience stands out'

The Daily Hitter

'The sheer mass of quality one-liners proved to be a dozen times more prolific than that of most current stand-ups and refreshingly free of any easy concessions to smut.'

Evening People

Lee Parsley, the laconic, drawling Canadian comedian with the postmodern one-liners, is set to return to the UK in July with his first-ever tour of Scotland. He will also appear in Wolverhampton, Plymouth and Birkenhead.

His one-off show in London in February was such a success, with rave reviews from Sultan B and Ben Merton among others, that we have dragged him back from his day job as a check-out clerk at 'Rocks – the outdoor store' to do fifteen more shows. His material includes surreal observations on the universe as well as regular weird stuff about his customers at the 'we'll keep you warm whatever the weather' retail outlet where he works.

The long-reigning Canadian king of the one-liner has written for many of the legendary Canadian talk-show hosts as well as having appeared as a one-armed bandit in Looking for Fruit and as a Rocky Mountain park ranger in The Bears Have It.

He's one of the funniest people ever to have come out of a condominium in Alberta, so if you would like to interview him for your magazine, please don't hesitate to get in touch.

Yours,

Dear Mr Devon,

We are writing to invite you to send a reporter and a photographer to cover the opening of our new Living Leather store in Wisbech next week. This will be of particular interest to your readers, 30% of whom live within walking distance of our new store.

The opening will take place on Monday 12 March at 10.30 a.m. and will be attended by local TV celebrity Barbie Perkins ('Susie' from Southenders). She will be wearing 'Cindy' – one of our new autumn range of all-in-one leather outfits.

Please let me know if you will be able to attend.

I look forward to hearing from you.

Yours sincerely,

DECLINING MEDIA COVERAGE

You may be asked to contribute to a radio or television programme in order to represent your company on an issue that concerns them and which is currently in the news. Most people are happy to participate in such discussions since they generate debate while simultaneously helping to give free publicity to your firm.

There may be the odd occasion, however, when you do not feel, for whatever reason, that it is appropriate for you to participate in such discussions, because you are busy, or because you are nervous of live debate, or because you know that your company's official position may be an unpopular one. In such circumstances, you should decline, but as politely as possible.

Always begin by thanking the organiser or producer for the invitation. Try to give as boring a reason as possible for not being able to attend and do express regret. Add that you hope there will be opportunities to appear on the programme in future – this sounds slightly less churlish and may even do you some good in the future.

Dear Joe,

Thank you for inviting me to appear on *Woodstock at One* in order to speak about our farming methods.

Unfortunately, I shall have to decline on this occasion because of unavoidable prior commitments. I know that this is a really important issue for a lot of local people and I would have very much liked to have been able to state my position clearly, but, as I say, this will not be possible this week.

I am sorry, but I hope that we may have the opportunity to work together on some future programme.

Best wishes,

LETTERS TO THE EDITOR

Whether you have a particular grievance against a newspaper that you wish to air or a more general problem with the world at large, you can always write to the newspaper in question setting out your complaint and hoping that the letter will be printed on the 'letters to the editor' page. Whatever your reason for writing, it is important to bear in mind that most serious newspapers receive many more letters than they can ever possibly print and yours will, therefore, need to be of particular interest if it is going to stand a chance of appearing in print.

You should also always bear in mind that space is limited, that your letter will undoubtedly be cut to fit the page and that no one will ask for your permission to do so. If your original is so wildly cut as to have its original meaning distorted, then a further letter may help matters, but it is generally better to try and keep your letter fairly short so that it cannot be cut at all.

Start by being assertive and stating the capacity in which you are writing the letter. If you are complaining about an article which referred to yourself or your company, state your position within the company and/or your area of expertise. Say how your business might have been adversely affected and what remedy you would like to see implemented – an admission of error correcting your first letter is the normal remedy.

If your complaint is not personal but about a particular article in the newspaper, be specific and quote the date on which the article appeared. Bear in mind that even a letter to a magazine with a relatively low circulation will be read by any number of experts in the relevant field. Check every detail in your letter because someone else is sure to notice if you get a point wrong. Never speak on behalf of other people if you do not have the necessary authority to do so and always be prepared to argue your point further if your letter gets a, possibly lengthy and highly critical, response.

PERSONAL LETTER

If an article has been written about your work which you consider has misrepresented your interests, then do feel free to complain but bear in mind that many people believe the old adage that 'any press is good press'. Try to maintain good relations with the newspaper in question, since you may wish them to cover some other aspect of your work in the future. It is silly to be unnecessarily touchy but if the errors are a genuine misrepresentation of your work and may cause you financial loss or embarrassment, do not hesitate to write. Address your letter to the editor and let it be as long as it needs to be, since you will have to note down every fault in the original article and then correct it. Be as clear and factual as you can and as unemotive as possible.

Dear Miss Thomas,

We are writing to complain about an article which appeared on page 3 of today's newspaper under the heading 'Station now a bargain basement shop' and which concerned the launch of our new range of products.

In this article you state that:

The station was completely closed while our fashion show took place.

All our clothes are only available in sizes 8 and 10.

Several of our models appeared to be anorexics.

The head of our personnel team is a former topless model.

All of the above statements are false. The facts are as follows:

The lobby of the station was closed to passengers but there were clear passageways signalled along either side of the platforms and all trains were running to schedule.

All our clothes are available in all sizes from 8 to 16.

All our models are in-house staff and, to the best of our knowledge, none suffers from an eating disorder.

The head of our personnel team worked as a greeter in a night-club for a period of two months eight years ago.

We appreciate your attempts to cover the opening of our new autumn range but would have preferred them to be accurate. I am sure that, now we have pointed out these unfortunate errors, you will print this letter in full so that your readers may also be fully informed about the real facts.

Yours sincerely,

SPECIFIC ARTICLES

If you feel that a specific article in a newspaper is biased or simply wrong, and you are sufficiently motivated, then write and say so but try to avoid sounding like a hysterical eccentric with nothing better to do. Be as objective and as concise as possible. Make your point and move on.

Dear Letters Editor,

I do not consider myself to be prudish and am certainly not an advocate of any form of censorship, but I am the father of two small children and was genuinely shocked by the gratuitous sadism and violence in the photographs which accompanied your article 'Show time' (23 March).

I have bought your newspaper for most of my adult life and value its coverage of both local and international issues, but really! To illustrate an article about the rush hour on the tube with such alarming, sensational and graphic photographs was both offensive and highly irresponsible. Beyond the mere unpleasantness of the photos themselves, they were also, clearly, not even taken at the station in question. There was, however, nothing in the text to indicate that this was not the case. I found this omission to be both insidious and misleading. On reading the article, I was faced with the added dilemma of having to explain these pictures to my children – which was particularly difficult given their irrelevance to the text.

If these photos had added an extra dimension of understanding to a news story, then, perhaps, I would have found them more acceptable. But they did not. I can only assume they were there to attract readers.

I was both upset and disappointed in this extraordinary lack of editorial judgement in a newspaper I have always considered to have avoided the worst excesses of the tabloid press.

Yours sincerely

GENERAL GRIEVANCE LETTER

The only really important guideline here is that unless you write immediately, your letter will be out of date and will never be published. As with the more specific letters, try not to be hysterical but rather to be

☞ Always write straight away to ensure your grievance letter is topical.

informative, factual and up to the minute. But also aim to keep your letter as interesting and snappy as possible – it will be competing with hundreds of others for space. Then post it immediately, including your full name and address.

SAMPLE LETTERS ALL ON THE SAME ISSUE:

(All of these appeared in the same newspaper on the same day, responding to the same article, giving some idea of the range of responses which might be published on one day. Notice the breadth of the spread and the evenness of coverage required).

Poor old Bertie Porter! How ridiculous that he should attempt to uphold the law. His on-the-spot fines policy will never work. The same was tried by imposing fines for smoking on trains or buses. Young people naturally paid no heed. Zero tolerance may have worked in New York but it will not work in London.

The *Evening News* is right to speak out with such 'passionate intensity' on this subject ('A dotty idea that leaves real crime untouched', 5 October) – and it is refreshing to find that it has a firm position on the question of pot (namely, that it is a delicate question, a matter of debate, and the focus of a review).

Is it right, then, that drugs and crime should be entirely ignored and the problem should be left to fester? Is it absurd to suggest that any government should interfere? You can be confident that the present prime minister is unlikely to do so.

S Burton, London W5

I am against politicians laying down what kind of lifestyle we should lead, particularly when the advice is the 'do as I say, not as I do' variety. Bertie Porter tells us that the preferred Tory model of living is a man and woman married and with children. Since he himself does not conform to the model, why should anyone else feel they have to, unless they so choose?

R Tutton, London E7

With reference to the *Evening News's* article on Bertie Porter and his on-the-spot fines ('A dotty idea', 5 October), once again I feel I must point out that your newspaper is caught up in a popular misapprehension when it links the words 'cannabis' and 'drugs'. As any scientific report shows, cannabis is not a drug, a drug being that which alters the cell structure of the body, perverting those cells into needing the drug to survive. Unlike tea, coffee, alcohol and cigarettes, which do, and are, drugs. Let's keep the record straight.

B Scutty

Secretary

Campaign for Real Information on Drugs

As a Tory voter, I find Bertie Porter's views on cannabis and his zero tolerance to be outdated. I abhor any drug, hard or soft, but I abhor out-of-date or out-of-touch politicians, too, particularly those of the dinosaur mould. As far as I can see, the present Tory party is not that much changed from the old lot. As a constituent of Marty Prattle – whom I did not vote and would never vote for – I would prefer, reluctantly, to put up with another term of Tommy Blokey and co. than another government of unreconstructed Conservatives. If William Haggis sincerely aspires to be prime minister, he should sideline, marginalise, or preferably ditch Mr Porter altogether, for until he does, he and the party will be quite unacceptable and not electable for a very long time.

C Tetterdine, London SW3

Whatever your point of view, do bear in mind the laws of defamation and libel (see Chapter 9).

9

LEGAL
MATTERS

- LIBEL
- YOUR RIGHTS
- COPYRIGHT
- WITHOUT PREJUDICE
- COMMUNICATION WITH SOLICITORS
- THREATENING LEGAL ACTION

A written letter is an obvious contender for legal action for the simple reason that the evidence is right there before the potential litigant's eyes. The existence of the statement cannot be denied, since it is there for everyone in court to see. There are three main areas where the law might affect your letter:

1 Defamation (the damaging of someone's reputation in writing).

2 Copyright (the copying of someone else's work).

3 Contractual matters (signing a statement which is deemed to constitute a written contract).

Any correspondent needs to have some basic idea of all these concepts if he or she is not to be caught up in time-wasting and costly legal action.

LIBEL

Many letters are written which, legally, might constitute grounds for libel or defamation but about which nothing further happens. Still, it is better to have some awareness of the law in this area rather than be caught up in a lengthy and costly legal process.

In terms of letters to the editor, most newspapers nowadays have a team of lawyers whose job it is to sit and read proofs of every single item that gets into the paper, in an effort to ensure that nothing libellous is actually printed. Even lawyers, however, are not infallible and there will still be the odd article or letter which will manage to slip through the net. Try to avoid this one exception being yours.

'Libel' is written and 'slander' is spoken – together, these concepts comprise the two aspects of the word 'defamation'. A defamatory statement is one which in writing, art, recording or broadcast material insults the reputation of the subject of the statement.

Defamation is not a criminal offence. It is a civil offence but one of the rare civil offences which can be tried by a judge and a jury – and one for which legal aid is not available, however poor or deserving you might be. This lack of legal aid means that no one will bother to sue you unless they are wealthy, but it also means that their reputation will, consequently, be worth a lot more if ruined – so if you lose the case, the costs may be crippling. Though the Defamation Act 1996 made some difference to the situation by introducing a fast-track procedure for claims of under £10,000, it has yet to be seen how this may affect the situation in the long run. Always bear in mind, as stated above, that *any* form of your work may constitute libel, including email. Email libels are increasingly ending up in court, so take this threat seriously.

HOW A LIBEL ACTION HAPPENS

For there to be any valid claim, the material has to have been published. This may sound obvious, but it should be pointed out that the definition involves some element of public display. The easiest way to avoid being sued, therefore, is to address a letter of complaint to an individual and then to mark both the letter and the envelope 'private and confidential'. The upside of this course of action in a letter to the editor, for example, is that you will not be sued but the downside is that your letter will never be published, rather defeating the point of the exercise. The best course to follow is to use your common sense. If your letter seems unnecessarily rude and personal, then you probably shouldn't be sending it anyway.

STANDARDS OF PROOF

It must be proved that your statement has harmed someone's reputation or has caused that person to be shunned in the opinion of right-thinking members of the community. This definition will, therefore, cover all references to dishonesty, immorality or, even, the suggestion that someone has a contagious disease. These references, it should be noted, need not be explicit. Anything that can be inferred from your statement, however oblique, may constitute libel.

It is also, generally speaking, necessary to be alive to sue for libel – but, when speaking ill of the dead, do bear in mind that other, still living, people may be implicated in your statements. If stating that '*Mr Jones was part of a fine tradition of train robbers, in a family in which this profession has always been handed down from generation to generation*', even if Mr Jones is now deceased, do make sure that he has no living offspring, since they may validly claim that this statement has libelled them, too.

Practically speaking, try to make your claim as general and as unspecific as possible, unless you are completely sure of your facts and prepared to argue them at your own expense.

DEFENCES

Most importantly, it doesn't matter what you say as long as it is true. If you can prove the truth of your statement, then this is a complete defence and that is the end of the matter. If, however, you wrote what you thought was probably true, even in good faith, and it turns out to have been false, then you may be found guilty. It is up to you to prove that what you have said is true. It may well *be* true, but if you cannot prove it, you will lose the case.

You may also be able to claim fair comment, which exists to defend freedom of speech and is most frequently used by journalists. If your statement is based upon correct facts and was not motivated by malice, then you may have an absolute defence. If it can be proved, however, that you have just been involved in bitter divorce proceedings with the subject of your public letter, for example, then malice may well be hard to dispute.

A special defence may be available if you can prove that your words were used in all innocence. If you did not know, or could not have known, that your statement would offend anyone, then an 'offer of amends' may be an appropriate remedy.

The most useful general advice in this area of the law, however, is that old adage 'if in doubt, leave it out'.

YOUR RIGHTS

A contract need not always be a signed document, although, by definition, a letter is likely to be a fixed statement of words with a signature at the bottom.

Any contract requires '*offer*' and '*acceptance*' with '*consideration*' in order to be binding. 'Offer' and 'acceptance' are self-evident but 'consideration' means something of value that has been transferred from one party to the other, in order to validate the contract. If you are offered some work on the telephone, for example, and then write back to the client repeating what has been said, stating that you are about to start work on the project and adding the phrase 'just to confirm our discussion', then you will have a binding contract. The consideration will be the work you have done in exchange for the promise of money. If you are constantly receiving oral offers of work, it is probably a good idea to have a stash of these 'confirmation in writing' letters all ready to send off when required. Bear in mind, however, that you cannot unilaterally impose terms – you can only repeat and reiterate whatever exact terms you and the employer agreed over the telephone. Any new terms you add into your letter ('I have four weeks to finish this work' when no time scale has previously been mentioned, for example) will only be legally binding if the employer writes back to you confirming this period of time.

> ☞ Writing to confirm an agreement discussed over the phone can pay dividends in the long run.

Remember that the terms of a contract work both ways. If you make a written offer in a letter, then you may well be held to the terms of this by the recipient. If in any doubt, you can always head your letter 'subject to contract' in order to clarify that you do not wish to be bound at this stage in the negotiations.

Your signature at the bottom of a letter confirms that it is definitely you who is making the offer or the acceptance, and not an agent. Once you have signed, you have a legally binding document, so consider your signature a valuable commodity and do not abuse it.

COPYRIGHT

There are two different areas where the laws of copyright might affect your letter:

1 Letters written by you containing your original ideas and words which you do not wish to be copied by anybody else.

2 Statements contained within your letters which may be deemed to have been directly copied from somebody else's work.

Both of these need some attention.

YOUR COPYRIGHT

Copyright can arise automatically through the mere act of setting words to paper. You do not have specifically to apply for copyright in your written material since it is vested in you as soon as it is written down. If you are writing a letter on behalf of an employer, however, the copyright naturally vests in the firm, not in you. If you are merely noting down your thoughts on paper in a general kind of way, however, this cannot be deemed to have created a copyright idea. You do not have legal protection over mere ideas.

Copyright is a 'civil' action. However blatant the copying, it is not a crime to reproduce your words in another forum. It may, however, be a civil offence and the offender may be liable to pay you damages. You may also be able to take out an injunction (a legal order that stops someone doing something), preventing that person from copying your work any more. Copyright in your work will remain vested in you or your family for seventy years after your death.

Inserting the familiar symbol '© 2000 by Joe Bloggs' at the bottom of any letter containing original material is not strictly necessary in English law, but may be worth doing when in doubt.

OTHER PEOPLE'S COPYRIGHT

As other people have a duty not to copy your work, so you have a legal duty not to copy other people's. If you wish to quote something that someone else has said or written, bear in mind the following points:

- Is the material factual, news or public information?

- If not, do you know who the author is?

- Has the author been dead for seventy years?

- If not, have you requested permission from that person, or their agent, to copy their work?

Bear in mind that lists of information or data compiled by other people may be copyright material, even if the information itself is well known. You cannot use someone else's database without getting permission.

If you are writing a letter for academic purposes, however, *and no money is involved*, then you may claim 'fair dealing' for research purposes. Even here, the use of more than a small sample of work may constitute an infringement of copyright. As a general guideline, quoting too long a section of someone else's text is probably a bad thing. Also remember that, whether or not the work is copyright, it is always a good idea to acknowledge your sources.

WITHOUT PREJUDICE

This is a much abused expression but should really only be used before litigation starts. If you add 'without prejudice' to the top of a letter, it simply means that the letter is not necessarily your final position on the matter. The use of the phrase enables the writer to state a particular, possibly temporary, position without necessarily implying that legal action is imminent. It does not, however, rule legal action out.

Dear Mr Stockley,

WITHOUT PREJUDICE

On 3 October you installed a new printer at our office. Since that date the printer has simply failed to print the required documents on four separate occasions. The paper feed has jammed on almost every occasion we have tried to use the machine and the letters, on the infrequent occasions on which they appear, are splattered with ink.

This is clearly a most unsatisfactory state of affairs. We can only assume, at this stage, that you have sent us a faulty machine and would be grateful if you could remedy matters immediately by sending someone to replace it and install a new printer.

Unless this matter is handled with some urgency, we shall not be able to keep up with our workload and shall lose both regular work and prospective work.

We trust we shall hear from you shortly,

Yours sincerely,
Helen Jones

RESPONSE

Dear Miss Jones,

WITHOUT PREJUDICE

Thank you for your letter of 13 October.

I am sorry to hear that you have been experiencing some teething problems with our Supreme Double-Luxe Printer. We have already instructed an engineer to attend at your office tomorrow morning.

This particular printer has already been successfully installed in a large number of businesses like your own. Feedback from your industry has been almost universally good. The few problems that have been experienced by our customers have all stemmed from computer software problems and I am therefore sure that our engineer will be able to sort this matter out to everybody's satisfaction.

Yours sincerely,

Philip Stockley

COMMUNICATION WITH SOLICITORS

Always try to resolve the situation orally before resorting to any others means of communication. Establish accurately what the problem is and see whether the situation can be salvaged. Always try telephoning and negotiating before any further action is taken. If this is not possible, try writing one letter, or getting a solicitor to write one letter, putting your position firmly but politely and in a legal, non-hysterical manner. This approach may yield dividends since nobody wants to go to court. A negotiated out-of-court settlement is always better for all parties. It avoids legal costs, embarrassment and unwelcome publicity. Always include copies of any relevant correspondence or correspondence referred to in your letter. Do not include any unconnected details or long-winded explanations as to why you are now attempting to deal with the matter on a legal basis. All this is irrelevant and will weaken your case. Simply state the problem, demonstrate your evidence and, if appropriate, state what you want to see done to resolve the issue.

> ☞ Settling disputes out of court avoids expensive legal costs.

Similarly, after receiving a letter threatening action from a firm of solicitors, do not be immediately terrified into submission. It may all be an elaborate bluff on the part of their clients. If you have a good case, then it does not matter if you are not familiar with legal terminology – everyone understands this and all courts of law will bend over backwards to accommodate you. Any letter of response that states simply and firmly your correct and truthful position will be absolutely sufficient to answer your case.

Dear Madam,

Re: Our Client: Print-a-Pront

We have been consulted by Print-a-Pront who are the contractors pursuant to a supply agreement for servicing equipment dated 23 May 2003.

You will note from the contract (clause 3.1) that the final date for payment by yourself for the amount is 14 days from the date of issue of the Certificate. You will further note that pursuant to the contract (clause 3.3.1) where you do not give written notice to the contractor within five days after the issue of the Certificate of any amounts that you propose to withhold and the grounds for so doing then you shall pay the amount stated as due on the Certificate. If, which is not admitted, your letter of 16 July 2003 provides the necessary notice and grounds, clearly it was not given within the required time, i.e. by 1 July 2003. In those circumstances you have no grounds for making any deductions from the sum certified and accordingly unless a cheque made payable to this firm is received on or before 15 August 2003 we shall advise our client that proceedings should be commenced against you.

We await your response.

Yours faithfully,

RESPONSE

Dear Sirs,

I am writing in response to your letter of 1 August 2003.

As you point out in your letter, the date by which notice had to be given was 1 July 2003.

We wrote to Print-a-Pront clearly stating why we were going to make the deductions on 15 May, 1 June and 20 June 2000 as well as on 16 July 2003.

Please find enclosed photocopies of the relevant letters as well as a small proportion of the voluminous correspondence between ourselves and your client regarding this matter. I would draw your attention in particular to our letters of 15 May and 1 June.

All of these letters were sent by recorded post and many were also faxed to your client.

Yours faithfully,

THREATENING LEGAL ACTION

This will almost invariably be because of unpaid bills. If you are unable to resolve a matter on the telephone, send a letter setting out your claim and warning that you are about to commence proceedings. It should be similar in style to a regular reminder letter and you need to sound polite but persistent and, above all, determined.

It should be signed by someone as authoritative as possible and sent by first-class, recorded post. You should state what will happen if your debt is not settled and you must be prepared to follow your threat through – if you do not, the client will never pay and may inform other clients that they do not need to pay either.

Dear Mr Thomas,

Account no 56789

We wrote to you on 1 September and 16 September, asking you to settle this account in the sum of £345.00. This sum is now over three months overdue.

We have received no response from you and must now insist that this sum is paid in full no later than 1 October.

If we do not receive this sum from you by 1 October, we shall commence legal action against you to recover our debt, as well as full legal costs.

Yours sincerely,

This may well do the trick. If it does not, however, you will be forced to follow it up with another, even more forceful letter. It is evident that you are not going to be paid, if the debtor can avoid doing so, and only the threat of imminent legal action may have any result now. Keep your last letter before action as matter-of-fact as possible, since it may appear in evidence in court. State simply what the debt is, how long you are giving the debtor to pay and be very specific that no further correspondence will be written before legal action is taken. There is no need to add extra threatening language – if the debtor is going to pay you, they will now. If they are not, you will have to go to court to sort the matter out anyway, so there's no point wasting your ink.

Dear Mr Thomas,

Account no 56789

You have ignored our letters of 1, 16 and 25 September, asking you to settle this account in the sum of £345.00 which was due to us on 20 June 2003.

I write to notify you that a County Court summons is being issued against you on 20 October for £345.00 plus costs.

If you wish to resolve this matter, you must forward a cheque to us for this sum within the next 24 hours.

No further notice will be issued to you.

Yours sincerely,

You could instruct a solicitor at this point, but this will cost money and may not be necessary. Bearing in mind that a court will expect both parties to have done all they reasonably can to settle matters before proceedings are begun, and that there is absolutely no point suing if you know that your debtor has no money with which to pay you, then you can now go to court to claim your debt.

As long as your claim is under £15,000 you can go straight to the County Court to recover your money. Contact their office and they will help you. There's no need to be anxious or to write a letter. They will give you the correct claim form and they will help you to complete the boxes. If you get stuck, ask. If you don't know what to say, tell the truth. It is simple enough to get an order forcing the debtor to pay – always remember, however, that if someone has no money, they will never be able to pay you.

10

THE ELECTRONIC
AGE

- EMAIL
- WORLD WIDE WEB
- FAXES

The internet is a global phenomenon and electronically links millions of people. It was created by the US military in the 1960s as a way of enabling government researchers who were working on secret military projects to share computer files. By the 1990s millions of people all over the world were 'logged on' to this massive computer network.

The internet is, quite simply, the world's largest computer network and growing all the time. Many users in Britain now have free access to this communications network and can, electronically, speak to all the other billion or so users across the globe. Instantly.

EMAIL

Email (or electronic mail) is simply the term used to describe any letters sent from one computer to another using the internet. It is the most widely used function of the internet, with hundreds of millions of messages sent and received daily, and this number is growing all the time. The huge advantage of this system is that, however long or complicated your message might be, it is still charged at the rate of one local telephone call, whether you are sending your message to Mongolia, Madagascar or Margate.

In order to connect to the internet you will need, obviously, a computer and a modem. This is the device which converts the information on your computer into information which can be sent down a telephone line and then converts the response back into computer information. Most modems can now do this at a rate of 56 thousand bits per second but the real speed of access to the internet will depend on your telephone line itself. With a poor line, all the technology in the world won't make your reception any faster.

Whatever the technology available to you, however, you will still need a Service Provider. These give you access to the internet. Most computers now come pre-loaded with access to various providers and you can use these to log on to the one with which you think you will be happiest. There are more and more Service Providers (or ISPs) to choose from, and you will need to think about how and when you are likely to use the internet most in order to select the one for you. Some provide deals with free calls at certain periods of the day. This may seem like a good deal, but check the helpline costs, which may be exorbitant. Others will offer a comprehensive package for a certain amount of money per month which includes all telephone calls and all helpline services. If you are intending to surf the web all day and all night, this may be a better deal for you.

An ISDN is a line which replaces your modem with a Terminal Adapter. The Adapter is, at the time of writing, expensive, and the quarterly rental charges may be enormous, but the situation is constantly, and rapidly, changing, so it is always worth enquiring with your local telephone company about the latest deals and any special packages that are currently on offer.

EMAIL ADDRESSES

Before you can send a message, you will need to know the recipient's address, which may be referred to as a User ID, an address or a name.

An email address consists of

name@ site. address The name is usually based on the user's real name. Though it needn't be. It could be anything, of course, but it is most likely to be something like:

johnt@aol.com After the user name, you will see an '@' sign, which separates the name from the site address. The site address will normally consist of the name of your Service Provider plus either a dot.com address or the initials of the country from which the email is being sent:

johnt@aol.co.uk If John Thomas was in Germany, for example, his address might be:

johnt@aol.co.de

(with *de* standing for 'Deutschland', of course).

It may be, however, that by the time our John Thomas tried to set up an account with aol, several other people also called John Thomas had already done so. This is why you might see an address like:

johnt25@aol.com or even:

john_t@aol.com Basically, anything will do as long as no one has used it already.

When choosing your own name, do try to be sensible. Your name, presented in a straightforward manner, is always going to be the best idea. It may seem funny to use a pet name when you log on, and many people do use these since they still think of email as a kind of computer game, but, in the long run, bear in mind that you will use your email for serious work correspondence and you may not wish your prospective clients to know that your girlfriend's nickname for you is:

reallybigjohn@aol.com When sending email, do remember that it is important to type exactly the right address. If you put the dot in the wrong place or write: *john-t* with a hyphen when the address should actually have been *john_t* with an underscore, then the message will, quite simply, not get through. Or, even worse, it may get through to completely the wrong person. It is important, therefore, to be absolutely accurate when taking down addresses. Bear in mind, also, that addresses are typed with no spaces between characters and no full stop at the end.

You will need to set up your email system before you can start to use it. This is normally a straightforward set of on-screen instructions, but, whatever system you are working with, you may well see references to your *POP account*. This stands for 'Post Office Protocol account' and refers to a storage 'post office' at your server's computer which will hold your messages for you until you log on to receive them. The only reason you need to know this is that, when the occasional problem occurs, your screen may show a message like 'could not connect to POP account', which normally means, in effect, 'try again later'. If you still cannot receive your messages, you may have to call an appropriate helpline.

When choosing an email address and server, do bear in mind that some addresses will only work from your own computer at home or in the office, while other systems can be picked up from the web itself and can thus be used anywhere in the world, in any cybercafe. This is why Hotmail is so popular with backpackers. Instead of having a personal log-on via Outlook Express, you can go into any café, log on to Microsoft Network – which, naturally, every computer in the world can reach – and then click on the 'mail' icon. All you need to remember is your password and, hey presto, you can read your messages. It's magic!

WEB TIP *Many of the big servers are starting their own web-based sites. Hotmail is the most popular, but btinternet has a system called Talk21, and you can also use any number of Search Engines, including **Yahoo.com** and **AltaVista.com**. It is a bit tedious having to set up the entire home page merely to pick up two messages, but these web servers can be very handy if you travel a lot or work away from your desk.*

USING EMAIL

PASSWORDS In order to access your account, so that your computer can check your POP account for mail, you will need to enter a password. People normally use their dates of birth or their children's names for this purpose. You can generally instruct your computer to save your password so that you don't have to remember it each time you log on, but it's a good idea to use a password that you can remember easily, just in case of emergencies.

You can tell your computer to check your POP account automatically on a regular basis. Or you can configure it to send messages from one address (e.g. your office address) and receive messages somewhere else (e.g. your home address). Clearly, the permutations are endless.

ACKNOWLEDGEMENT OF RECEIPT An increasingly frequently used email service is an 'attachment' which means that every email you send automatically has a footnote which asks the recipient to send this footnote back as soon as they have read and received the message in question. This is a particularly useful device when using email for business purposes because your computer may say that your email has been sent successfully but, as we have seen from potential address problems, it may not have been received. There could be a number of reasons for this: the particular address you used may be someone else's; the addressee has a new server; there is a software complication. Whatever the problem, this automatic footer is the email equivalent of 'recorded delivery' and is probably well worth investigating.

NEW MESSAGE When you want to send an email, draw down the email software's icon and click on the appropriate box, i.e. 'new message'. What you will see on most screens is quite similar at this stage:

TO: This is the address of the person to whom you are sending a message. If you are using the same online service as another member of that service, then you do not need to type in their full address, merely their account name: *johnt*, for example, if you are also using aol. If, however, your Service Provider is different, then you need to enter the full address.

CC: You can automatically copy your message to any number of people. Unless you are sending instructions for something very public, like how to get to a team football match, the Cc: function must be used with some sensitivity. It may be that you are sending a round-robin business message to various people who do not yet know each other's addresses. If you have not asked all the recipients whether they mind if all the other recipients know their address, then you should not use the Cc: function.

BCC: If in doubt, this is the polite option. It is used to send a copy of your message to someone, but this person will only know the name of the person to whom the original message was sent. The original recipient, however, will not see the names of the Bcc: recipients.

Inbox			subject ⧻ starts with ⧻
From	Subject	Sent	
Jollys Cabaret	Cabaret listings	11/10/00 18:38	
John Thomas	What band is your team?	11/10/00 18:33	
WriteNow	Re: two main thoughts	10/10/00 14:47	
Emily Sugar	hello, hello	10/10/00 10:32	
Luke Barten	re: materials update	10/10/00 10:24	
rupert_brown@priv ..	re: meeting at Talbot's	10/10/00 10:09	
andrewmondel	novel	09/10/00 19:43	
slaney.morris@lucky..	there you are	09/10/00 17:53	

ILLUSTRATION 9   Typical email inbox where new messages appear and can be stored

SUBJECT: Some systems will not send a message until you have entered a header into the 'subject' box. It is a good idea to use a header, since the whole idea of email is ease and speed of communication and, with a good header, the recipient should immediately know exactly what your message is about. If it is the first few words of a sentence, however, you can run straight on into the blank space below. You do not have to repeat these initial words in the main text. Your subject heading can be anything as long as it's clear and appropriate.

SAMPLE CASUAL SCREEN

From: slaney.morris@lucky   To: johnt@aol.com
Subject: There you are

Hey there! New job is good but v. hard work. Right now, I'm in tunnel vision mode, trying hard to impress my new boss.
I really meant to send you a message the other day to say what fun I had at the show last week. Your friend was really good. Next time, I must bring my friend, Lizzie, who would really enjoy it. You'd like her too -- she's a lot of fun.
See you soon and thanks.
Slaney

ILLUSTRATION 10 Email messages to friends are generally far more informal than any normal letter

Underneath the heading is a large, empty white box which is where you type in your message. Although most people use email extremely casually, without bothering to check their spelling and, quite often, without bothering with grammar or even punctuation, this is never wise. Try to think of email writing as regular letter writing, however brief that letter might be. Everything we have already learnt about writing a good letter applies just as well to computer messages and therefore good spelling, grammar and style will aid comprehension.

Do not leave the recipient confused. Try to be as clear as possible.
It may be brief, and the mere act of being able to send the message
in milliseconds means that people tend to write their messages in
milliseconds, but there's no point creating an unnecessary impression
that you are a sloppy person who might even be illiterate. This may
annoy people or, at worst, put them off working with you again.

SAMPLE FORMAL SCREEN

| From: rupert_brown@priv..   To: johnt@aol.com |
| Subject: re: Meeting at Talbot's |
| |
| Hi John! |
| I'll get back to you as soon as I can. |
| Best regards, |
| Rupert |

ILLUSTRATION 11   *Business email is less casual but still not usually as formal*
as a business letter

SEND Now you are ready to send. Look at the top of your screen and
there will be a box which says 'send'. Click on the box. If you are
currently logged on, the message will be sent immediately. If you are
not, then the message will wait in a queue in your outbox and go with
all your other messages as soon as you log on. If you press 'send', even
when you are not logged on, do try to remember that you have done so.
It may be that by the time you log on, you have already spoken to the
recipient and your message is now redundant. Or your position might
have changed but you have not changed your message. Just remember
that this is instant technology and, once sent, it may not be so easy to
cancel.

Your message is now in an electronic no-man's-land where it will
probably stay for the next few minutes. It may exist in this vacuum for

a few hours, or even a few days. Email is supposed to be instant communication but it is worth bearing in mind that a message may, on occasion, take as long as a week to reach its destination. Sometimes, particularly when sending a message abroad, the cables get blocked up or backlogged or simply overloaded. They will then send and receive messages gradually over the next few days. You should also not assume that, simply because you have sent a message, the recipient has seen it. He or she may not have logged on to the computer for a few days, or may simply have changed their email address and not be able to pick up messages at their former address. It is also true that email goes faster in the UK before lunch-time, since after America gets up and goes to work, the lines become a lot busier.

RECEIVE AND REPLY You may have a system which shows you in a corner of your screen that 'you have mail'. Or you may need to click on a box which will say something like 'send/receive'. You can normally print out your messages, save them, delete them or forward them straight to someone else. There is normally a function button for each of these commands and it is merely a question of clicking on the correct one.

If you want to reply to a message that you have received, you do not even need to know the sender's address. You simply read the message and then click on the box above, marked 'reply'. If you do this, the sender's message will automatically be incorporated at the bottom of your reply. This may be useful (if you want to remind someone what they have written, for example) or it may be unnecessary. Remember to delete the sender's message if you do not want it sent straight back to them. The original message and your reply will, of course, share the same subject heading, which can be a useful memory jog for the sender.

OTHER RESOURCES

ROUND ROBINS You can create a special 'round robin' mailing list which will contain the email address of everyone you know in a particular group: members of your hockey team, for example. Once you have created your list, you can put all the necessary addresses on to it and then send the message to this list. Everyone in your hockey team will immediately know that the next fixture is on Saturday 14th and this will save you a lot of boring telephone work.

ADDRESS BOOKS You will see the term 'address book' somewhere on your toolbar. In this you can store a person's email address and personal details and then, whenever you type in their name, their address will automatically appear on the *To:* line. The advantage of this is that you do not have to remember people's email addresses.

HOLIDAY MESSAGES Just like an answering machine, you can set up your email to respond automatically to all incoming messages with one of your own which states that you are on holiday and will be back on a particular date. This may be very useful and, unlike an answering machine, is not normally a security hazard since it does not mean that strangers will instantly know that your residence is ripe to be burgled (your email address, of course, does not identify your actual home address).

FORWARDING MAIL Most services will let you forward your email to another account straight away. The simplest way to do this is to ask your service to forward your email automatically to another address. If you want to forward a message you have received to someone else, you can simply copy the message, paste it on to a new message, add the prospective recipient's address and then press 'send'.

KEEPING IT SHORT

An email may be short but it is still a letter. Do not forget this. Try not to let all your standards of literacy drop just because you know you can create an email in seconds. Remember all your basic skills of spelling, punctuation and grammar. You can use accepted abbreviations, but

☞ Email is fast communication, so no one wants to read a long, rambling message.

don't try to be funny and make your own up. This is as much a business communication as any other and you should always try to create exactly the same impression as you would wish to if you were writing a conventional letter. With friends, of course, it isn't quite as important to use correct style, but even your best friend might find it a little odd that you suddenly don't know how to spell.

Keep it short. No one really wants to read a huge, long message on the screen. If it has to be lengthy, then of course make it so, but consider, if this is the case, whether a letter on paper might not be a better option. Since it is going to take the recipient a while to study the contents, they might not read your message carefully for a couple of days anyway, so the whole purpose of email is invalidated.

Keep it up-to-date. You can send a letter about the price of a product only to discover that the currency exchange rate has changed in the last hour, invalidating your first message. So send another one – that's what email is designed for.

Just because you can send it instantly doesn't mean that an email won't exist for ever, just as any letter on paper will. So think about what you really want to say and if you're not sure, wait. Don't just push the 'send' button because it's there. Your message may be read on screen, passed around someone's office or filed away indefinitely. There's no necessity to try to be humorous, super-casual or flippant just because you're using modern technology. If your message is so casual that you don't care, then maybe you're better off using the telephone, anyway.

INFORMALITY

Writing style in emails may not be as formal as that in a non-electronic letter. In practice, this means that some abbreviations and symbols have developed as a kind of standardised e-shorthand. If you choose to use this, do bear in mind that not everyone will automatically have the same knowledge of this system as you. Try to use only the symbols (or smileys) which you know the recipient will understand. Otherwise, this is just as rude as going to a business meeting and talking in French when you know that some participants at the meeting do not speak this language. Also, do bear in mind that while the smiley symbols themselves might be quite funny, this does not necessarily make your message funny. And even if the recipient finds it funny, this does not necessarily mean that they will not sue.

E-shorthand is possibly the fastest growing linguistic sub-strain in the 21st century, but it is, primarily, the language used by young people when writing emails or chatting in 'chat rooms' (see below). An increasing number of mobile and WAP phones also feature the ability to use this shorthand for short messages (SMS). Since it primarily consists of acronyms, which started off as a military device during the Second World War, it is perfect for the kind of small, digital screens that are becoming more and more common. Whether it's your own telephone bill or your company's, we all know that time counts, and costs, so obviously these acronyms have caught on in a big way. Just bear in mind all the general advice on informality above if you choose to use them.

COMMONLY USED SMILEYS

:-)	happy	:-(	sad
;-)	winking	:-o	shocked
8-)	glasses-wearing nerdy type	:-&	tongue-tied

COMMONLY USED ABBREVIATIONS

AFAICT	as far as I can tell
AFAIK	as far as I know
AFK	away from keyboard
AIUI	as I understand it
B4	before

BTW	by the way
BAK	back at keyboard
BBL	be back later
BRB	be right back
BTDT	been there, done that
BTW	by the way
cld	could
DILLIG	do I look like I give . . .
doc	document
EOF	end of file
FAQ	frequently asked question
FOC	free of charge
foll	following
FWIW	for what it's worth
FYI	for your information
GFETE	grinning from ear to ear
GR8	great
GTG	got to go
HTH	hope this helps
IDST	I didn't say that
IDTS	I don't think so
IIRC	if I recall correctly
IMHO	in my humble opinion

IMNSHO	in my not so humble opinion
IMO	in my opinion
IOW	in other words
ITRO	in the region of
KYPO	keep your pants on
LOL	laughing out loud
msg	message
NRN	no reply necessary
NW	no way!
OIC	oh, I see
OTOH	on the other hand
OTT	over the top
PD	public domain
PMFBI	pardon me for butting in
ROTFL	rolling on the floor laughing
RTFM	read the manual
SITD	still in the dark
TBD	to be discussed
TEOTW	the end of the world (as we know it)
TIA	thanks in advance
TNX	thanks
UGTBK	You've got to be kidding
VR	virtual reality

WCA	who cares anyway?
WRT	with regard to
YMMV	your mileage may vary
YOOC	you're out of control
YSYD	yeah, sure you do
YTTT	you telling the truth?
YYSSW	yeah, yeah, sure, sure, whatever

If you are going to use any of the above abbreviations, or, indeed, any of your own devising, then do be consistent. Don't type the phrase out in full, then use an abbreviation, then use the full phrase again. It looks odd. If you are going to try and maintain a casual writing style and use abbreviations, then don't suddenly start mixing this up with very formal language and phrases like 'therewith mentioned' or something similar. It just makes you look a bit silly.

SHOWING RESTRAINT

The whole idea of email is to facilitate communication and to keep it fast and instant. Bear this in mind. Do not be rude and glib just because you can.

It is in your own interests to be polite since anyone you work with, from a colleague to the most junior employee, will always respond better to a well-mannered request than a brusque, and possibly actionable, insult.

SAMPLE: POOR EMAIL

> Shakira,
>
> Let me have your opinion on the Sweetings Account ASAP. We discussed this at length last week and I haven't heard a word out of you since then. Are you in hiding? Have you gone AWOL? Are you alive? ASAP, I said.

No one will think this message is funny but it is the kind of message that email can propel you to write. It may even leave you open to legal action, so do think about it, before you write some supposedly witty, throw-away insult. Just because your message is instant doesn't make you a stand-up comic.

SAMPLE: BETTER EMAIL

> Hi, Shakira,
>
> I'm slightly concerned about the Sweetings Account. I know we looked at their figures together last week and we said that we would try to come up with a programme of action. I thought you said that you would do this by Monday but I know that you have been very busy in Manchester. Maybe you could take a break from that and spend a few days looking at the Sweetings figures instead since I think we should act on this ASAP. Do get back to me as soon as you have formed an opinion.
>
> Yours,
> Burt

ATTACHMENTS

Attachments need not be a complicated business. Basically, you can cut and paste the attachment into your main email text, using your word-processing software, and then send it as part of your message. This will work but is slow and you will almost certainly lose all your formatting. Or, alternatively, you can create an 'attachment file' which appears as a paper clip in the corner of the screen when the recipient receives your message. If you then click on the paper clip, the original message will disappear and all you will see will be the attached document.

If the other person is on the same server system as you, then you can insert almost anything into your message and it will go straight through. Problems begin to arise when two different servers are involved and one server cannot read the format of another. If you send pictures, for example, in the body of the text, it may corrupt them and the recipient will receive merely a confused series of images. This is why it may be better to use an attachment, which cannot be corrupted.

To create an attachment, you will have to use your server's 'file transfer' system and all of these are different. Most systems work by clicking on the 'file' menu to a command labelled 'send' and then choosing 'mail recipient'. Your file will then be attached and you will see the 'Outlook Express' picture come up and ask you to whom you wish to send the attachment. But not all service systems work this way. You may have to ring your server's helpline in order to work out how to do this the first time. After that, it will be straightforward!

Bear in mind that attachments can take a very, very long time to download. Sound and video clips can take hours, depending on the resolution and the length of the clip. You may feel it is essential that your friend at work witnesses a classic, messed-up hole-in-one but they may not find golf quite as hilarious as you – particularly not when it blocks their screen for half an hour.

E-ETIQUETTE

Email is instant. Every one knows that. You can send a casual message to your friend in Botswana and they will receive it straight away. It is therefore unforgivable not to reply to your emails. Even if this is merely to say: 'I'll get back to you as soon as I can'.

On the other hand, do bear in mind that it is always possible that your message has entered the ether and is now lost in space. You may feel mortified that your friend never got back to you about the party invitation, but it is just about possible that the message got lost. If in doubt, there's always the good old telephone.

WORLD WIDE WEB

The world wide web (or www) is not the same as the internet and is not strictly to do with letter writing, but it can be closely related to both of these functions so it is worth understanding. It is only one software system running on the internet but one that has become almost ubiquitous.

Its direct implications for letter writing are that you can now, almost invariably, enter someone's web page and then send and receive email from within that page. In other words, you can click on an address on the web page and write to that person without exiting your current screen, which, when you are looking at technical details and information, can be a very useful function.

The web itself is a system without boundaries. You can click on a link and you might be shown a document about an English railway line. Within this document, there might be a reference to Harry's Yorkshire Steam Line. If you then click on Harry's Line, you may enter his site without ever having requested his permission. Harry himself may have received a message from a rail enthusiast in India and this Indian address will then appear on your screen. Click on this and you might now be shown the railway timetable for a train from New Delhi to Bombay. And so on.

The possibilities are endless. You will not necessarily want to know the times of the domestic Indian trains, but you never know. Or your friend might want to know. And you could then send this web page name on to her and her email address is now directly linked to the original English railway line site. It's a mind-boggling business.

Whatever service provider you run, they will start by showing their introductory screen. This is called the home page. This will, almost certainly, have hundreds of links of its own, including several adverts. Always try to be aware of what is information on your home page and what is merely a paying advert. Try to think of your home page as a magazine with some news and features supplied by the publisher and some adverts paid for by other firms.

> ☞ **Learn to differentiate between adverts and info on web pages – it can save you time and money.**

USEFUL WEB TOOLS

BACK Takes you back to the previous screen.

HOME Takes you to your server's home page.

HISTORY Shows you a list of every site you have ever visited and the date on which you visited that site.

FAVOURITES This is a very useful device which allows you to bookmark pages that you think you might wish to look at again. If you click on 'favourites' or 'bookmark' while in an interesting site, you will then see a box inviting you to 'add'. Click on add and you will have created a favourite site which you can then file within a pre-existing list of potential headings already on your favourites list. These will generally include such obvious contenders as 'search engines', 'entertainment' and 'travel' but you can just as easily create your own folders. Using this method will make it infinitely easier to find a suitable site in future.

SEARCH You can enter a keyword or words and all the sites that list those words will be listed on your screen. Some of these may have nothing to do with the information you are looking for, but if you then click on each one, you can quickly see if this is the case.

GO Alternatively, if you know the exact address of the site that you are seeking, you can simply type this in at the 'Go' sign and the web will take you straight there. If you do not, you will have to enter those elements of its name that you do know under 'Search'.

NEWSGROUPS

Newsgroups are discussion groups. If you feel you need to have an electronic global debate about the best way to make an orchid grow in cold weather, then you need a newsgroup.

A newsgroup is a computerised system for leaving both public and private messages. Many private groups of friends have created their own newsgroups so that they can exchange information, while many professional organisations use newsgroups as a kind of electronic bulletin board, with every member posting up titbits of information as soon as they arise.

The main difference between using a 'round robin' system to copy your message to all your colleagues and a newsgroup is that, for a newsgroup, you will dial just one dedicated phone number and then you will be connected to all the BBSs (Bulletin Board Systems) within that service provider.

Useful addresses for public news servers might be found listed under:

WEB TIP
www.yahoo.com/News/Usenet/Public_Access_Usenet_Sites/

You may choose to 'chat' electronically to your fellow orchid-loving friends or to post your opinions on the best pop songs of the seventies or, more importantly, to write a note about your missing relative. All of these things are becoming more and more accessible, and global, all the time.

Most people will access their newsreader from Outlook Express, where it is simply a question of pulling down the 'newsgroups' dialogue box and then asking it to give you a list of all the newsgroups to which your service provider subscribes. If you are using Outlook Express, you simply look at this list, choose the newsgroup to which you would like to subscribe and then click the '*subscribe*' button. The first time you open any particular newsgroup, you will see all the messages from that group currently held by your service provider. Once you have clicked on them, and read them, they will probably not reappear next time you enter the newsgroup.

A newsgroup may be a useful way to exchange information. It may simply be an addictive, nocturnal activity. Or it may be both.

CHAT ROOMS

You may find your e-pals through regular email. There may be people with whom you start by exchanging regular communic-ations but to whom you end up writing snappy messages so frequently that they eventually become your e-pals and you find that your working day seems somehow slightly duller without a word from your friend.

It is possible that you will find your friend through a newsgroup.

WEB TIP *It is most likely, however, that you will find your brand new e-pal through the use of a chat room. Here, all the normal rules of letter writing may fall by the wayside. A new line of dialogue will flash up about once a second. There's no time for spelling things out, or even correctly. According to the 'Chatiquette' guidelines (outlined in greater detail at **www.ker95.com**), you should 'picture yourself entering a party. Don't worry about typing errors. They are expected, and can actually be a great source of laughter.' So, if it's friends and laughter you want, how do you begin?*

A chat room is not a place with voices and sound (or not generally yet, anyway) – it is a forum for written communication. The main difference between a chat room and regular email is that, when you are emailing a message to your e-pal, you send it and then carry on with your regular work. Later on in the day, possibly while you stop for a cup of coffee, you might be drawn to log on and see whether you have received a reply.

Chat, on the other hand, happens in what, in computer language, is called 'real time'. You type a message and someone else may reply instantly. You are, effectively, having an on-screen dialogue: the chat is being conducted via typing and not by speech.

The chat itself may happen in either a private or a group session. It's like going to a party where you don't know anyone and you're mingling in the general mêlée and then someone comes up to you and invites you to enter a side room with them for a one-to-one chat.

WEB TIP *Public chat rooms will often be used for public speaking or for a famous person to answer questions from all over the world while millions of other people look on. The public chat rooms provide (much-needed) revenue for many of the service providers, so you will tend to find that they are fairly easy to find – how you locate them depends on your service provider. Generally speaking, the easiest way is to enter the word* 'chat' *in your search box and then to search. Since most people will have access to MSN (Microsoft Network), it is worth noting that whether or not you subscribe to MSN, you can still enter any of its chat sites by selecting* **publicchat.msn.com** *and then clicking* 'OK'.

Do bear in mind that many, if not most, people now go to chat rooms in order to indulge in a spot of cybersex chit-chat. If it's advice from fellow orchid-growers that you're after, however tender you might like this advice to be, then you would be better off sticking with your designated newsgroup.

Genuine, and purposeful, uses for chat rooms, however, include international family reunions; groups planning international trips with participants from all over the world; and even international meetings for charity organisations who can swap useful information or get to know each other a bit more informally while still remaining in a fairly anonymous environment. Many colleges now use chat rooms to post lessons or even to conduct seminars. This may be a particularly useful, and constantly evolving, tool in disparate communities with poor access to transport facilities.

SELECTED TOOLS

WHO OR PEOPLE HERE Shows a list of all the people currently participating in the chat room session.

INVITE Allows you to invite a participant in the current public chat room to break off into a private chat room with you.

PROFILE Lets you view any information that the person with whom you are currently chatting has already made public. This will probably include that person's email address, although almost certainly not their real one.

CHANGE PROFILE Lets you amend or adapt the information that other people will see about you.

IGNORE Very usefully, allows you to block messages from a particularly irritating participant.

KICK Even more usefully, allows you to remove that participant from the chat room entirely – but only if you were the person who set up the chat room in question.

FAXES

Fax, or facsimile, is another way of sending a document instantly, using a telephone line. Fax machines normally look like telephones and can be used to make regular calls. Inside the machine, however, is a device which can photograph a document, convert it into a digital form for transmission, and then send this digital form down a telephone line to another fax machine somewhere else.

Despite the existence of email, businesses still fax documents frequently. If you do not have a scanner, then you will have to use your fax machine to send complicated images and photographs. If you do have a scanner, however, even this task can now be accomplished by your computer.

Sending a fax tends to be a lot slower than email but you do not need to know how to use a computer to send one. You also know that a fax will be seen in hard copy instantly and that it will not remain sitting 'inside' someone's screen until they decide to check their mail.

The fax machine may wane in popularity, but while they are still in use you should bear the following points in mind:

- It is very easy for the different pages of a fax to get separated at the other end of the line and you must take this into account. Telephone lines quite frequently get cut off in mid-connection and if someone else rings before you reconnect, the two, quite separate, faxes will become hopelessly muddled. There is a perfectly simple solution to this problem – always number your pages.

- Always include a cover sheet. The cover sheet should state the name of the sender, the name of the intended recipient, the date of transmission and, most importantly, the number of pages sent. This figure is usually expressed in the format: '2 (+ cover page)'.

- Even where the main body of the fax is typewritten, it is perfectly acceptable for the cover sheet to be a handwritten note. You can generally find a 'wizard' or model for a fax cover sheet within the software of your computer. In case you cannot, they would normally look something like this:

<u>Message by fax</u>

To:	Josephine Dillon, Dillon Textiles
Fax No:	01887 567 483
From:	George Buttle, Trade Cloths Ltd.
Fax No:	020 876 5432
Date:	24 January 2003
Pages:	3 plus cover sheet
Re:	Samples and swatches

Dear Josephine

Here is the information about the swatches you
requested.

I'll be in Bartle tonight so do try me on the mobile
(07982 765 432) until 10 pm if you need to know
anything else.

Yours sincerely

11

FILING

CORRESPONDENCE

- FILING

- KEEPING COPIES

- DATA PROTECTION ACT

- CREATING AN ARCHIVE

Every business receives and sends a huge amount of post every day. Most of this correspondence is eventually filed away in order that it can be found when required. Any letter may remain in these archive files for years and any letter you have sent will, equally, be stored by you in case anyone needs to contact you about this material.

You simply never know when a letter you wrote three years ago might suddenly be relevant – for research purposes, or indeed for a law suit. It is a very good idea to give some thought to how you file your letters, both incoming and outgoing, and to how you are going to organise these files.

FILING

Filing is the storing of documents in a systematic way so that they may easily be retrieved at a later date for reference purposes. This retrieval system may be as simple as one large box or it may be a huge, electronically controlled system, but all systems, however straightforward, should demonstrate the following characteristics:

SIMPLICITY It should be easy to follow and simple to use. It should be as easy for your colleague to locate one of your letters as it is for you. Using your own idiosyncratic system – like filing under years of major events in your life – may be fun for you but will be absolutely impossible if anyone has to step into your shoes and take over.

SECURITY All valuable letters should be secure. Whether this is as straightforward as leaving them on the top shelf, away from your infant children's prying hands, or as complex as a locked vault, the same principle applies.

CROSS-REFERENCE SYSTEM If you mark all your letters as you receive them with all possible relevant cross-references, this will make life much simpler for you later on.

APPROPRIATE CLASSIFICATION SYSTEM Most people put their letters into files. If you realise that you are going to receive an awful lot of correspondence on one particular topic, it is worth creating a file for this topic alone. Once you have several files, there are various ways in which you might store them as a whole:

- Alphabetical.
- Numerical.
- Thematic.
- Geographic.

ALPHABETICAL

This is the most common way to file letters in business. If you are subsequently looking for a letter, you can simply go to the file with the correct initial and find the file. It will help if you put alphabetical separators in the files so that you know where each alphabetical letter finishes and the next one starts.

Of course, problems will always arise when you are trying to decide under which letter of the alphabet you should file any one piece of correspondence. If you receive a letter from Fred Potter of Unigrumble, for example, does this go under F, P or U? If you are going to spend more time worrying about this than writing your next letter, then this is probably not the system for you.

For those who do choose an alphabetical system, people are generally filed under surnames. Organisations are normally filed under the first word that distinguishes that organisation from all other organisations.

EXAMPLE

Diocese of Swindon	under 'D'
Borough Council of Epping	under 'E'
Chamber of North-Eastern Commerce	under 'N'

NUMERICAL

If you have a vast amount of correspondence on an enormous range of subjects, the huge advantage of a numerical system is that you are not going to run out of numbers. Its disadvantage will be that you will not automatically know where to find your letter. If you use this system, you will also need a file which shows you what number refers to which topic. This is clearly going to be quite a lot of work so it's probably only worth doing in a large corporation.

THEMATIC

Most home businesses store their letters thematically. You might, for example, have one file named 'house' in which you have individual sections called 'electricity', 'telephone' and 'mortgage'. It will clearly be slightly quicker to find these sections if they are divided by coloured separators.

You may then have several 'work' files – one for each project you have worked on, perhaps, or one running from the beginning of each tax year to its end. This last system is very practical since it also gives you a date-marker and if, in future years, you need to look something up, you will generally have some idea of when this event happened and when, therefore, you received the letter. Then it is merely a question of looking through that year's file.

GEOGRAPHIC

This is generally only a relevant system if your work takes you all over Britain, and perhaps the rest of the world. If this is so, then it may be very handy at a later date. You may receive a request for a job in North Wales and then, instantly, be able to look up all other correspondence you have had from this area of Britain. This may well jog your memory about both the location and the people you worked with previously in that location. This may well influence your decision about whether you wish to work in North Wales, for example, again.

KEEPING COPIES

For all sorts of common-sense reasons, it is worth keeping a copy of every letter you write. These days, this is generally not a problem since they will all be stored on the hard disc of your computer, but you may want to keep them as hard copies which may be more instantly accessible.

Anything that might have some future legal repercussions should always be kept indefinitely. Any letter that relates to a tax matter should also be kept. If the letter is about a specific issue, such as the challenging of a parking fine, for example, there is little point keeping a copy of your correspondence on the matter once this has been resolved one way or the other. If, on the other hand, you think that you may well be writing many more such letters in the future, challenging your parking fines in similar circumstances, then, of course, it will save you time to have a copy of your previous letter.

Use your common sense and your discretion.

SECURITY & DATA PROTECTION ACT, 1984

All records have a security aspect. Most people are sensitive about how much they earn and do not want all their colleagues to share this information with them. Letters you have written to, or received from, prospective employees about salaries, therefore, are bound to have a security aspect. Similarly, they may contain private information about these prospective employees' past employment, reasons for leaving their current job and relationships with their current employers.

All this information may suddenly become startlingly relevant in the future when this person's former boss has become a public figure in a high-profile celebrity job. Since much of this personal information will have been stored inside a computer data bank, anyone who knows a thing or two about 'hacking' will immediately be able to dig out all sorts of pertinent information and do what they like with it, including selling it to the press.

The Data Protection Act, 1984 was created to counteract people's more general fears about these risks. All those who keep computerised records are required to register with an office called the Data Protection Registry. They then need to state why they need the records and what use they intend to make of them. They also need to prove that they are operating an entirely secure system.

The Act lays down certain 'data protection principles' and failure to uphold these principles may lead to your name being removed from the Data Protection Registry. It is then an offence for you to hold any records on a data bank in the future. The main principles are:

- Data which has been obtained lawfully and fairly may be recorded.

- Data may only be held for the reasons given on the registration document.

- Data must be sufficient but not excessive and it must be kept up to date.

- Data may not be disclosed for any other reason than that which is stated on the registration document.

- Data should not be stored for any longer than is necessary for the purpose stated.

- Any individual may know what records are kept on him or her and is entitled to have access to these records without delay.

- The system must be secure.

CREATING AN ARCHIVE

In the future, when you've forgotten all about it, a letter you wrote may suddenly become either useful or valuable. For these reasons, consider making a little more effort than simply putting your letters in a file, by creating an archive. This is a filing system which enables you instantly to access *and view* old materials. Archives are storage systems which may be used for display purposes. If you have several treasured letters from a deceased grandparent, for example, you could put them into an album alongside photos of that grandparent and any other treasured memorabilia. Tickets from shows you all saw together, for example, or the menu from your grandfather's eightieth birthday party.

In fifty or a hundred years' time, letters that you have written might take on a similar emotional value for your grandchildren and it is worth considering keeping your own personal correspondence for this purpose.

Bear in mind, when storing paper and photographic material, that these are delicate materials. Paper may fade and rot; photographic paper may fade and the image disappear. It is really important, if you are going to create an archive, to take some time to study preservation techniques. If you do not, there will be nothing left for your grandchildren to study.

12
POSTAGE

- ENVELOPES

- TYPES OF POSTAGE

- POSTE RESTANTE

- FORWARDING MAIL

- SMALL PACKETS

- PRIVATE MAIL SYSTEMS

Generally speaking, letters are sent inside envelopes and the two should match up. Of course, no one really cares if you send a personal letter in a brown envelope and, in these days of recycling and environmental concern, a used brown envelope may gain you the most credibility points.

In business, however, it is best to bear in mind that image still counts. It may be that the person to whom you have addressed the letter will never actually see the envelope, since this will be opened in a mail room five storeys down. You should not, however, count on this.

ENVELOPES

Like paper, envelopes come in many different sizes, colours and qualities. You should choose a size which allows you comfortably to insert your letter into your envelope with the minimum of folds. Any fold on a letter makes that part of the letter slightly less legible. If you can avoid folding the letter over text, then you should try to do so.

If you don't want to fold an A4 letter, then you will have to use a C4 envelope. C5 envelopes involve folding a sheet of A4 down the middle once. Almost all business letters, however, are folded twice, equally, and then put into an envelope which is a standard 100mm by 220mm. It might sound over-fussy, but it does look neater if you fold the letter so that the sides are perfectly aligned. If you do not, it may well be completely crumpled by the time it gets to the recipient.

The Royal Mail uses a method of electronic sorting for any letters up to a certain weight and within a certain size range. These ranges are known as POP sizes and include any envelopes larger than 90mm by 140mm and smaller than 120mm by 235mm. They should also weigh less than 60g.

Bear in mind that if you are using the kind of business envelopes that have transparent windows, you should pay attention to folding your letter correctly, otherwise the address will be illegible.

ADDRESSING AN ENVELOPE

UK If you are writing to a UK address, you should, of course, include the full postcode. If you do not know it, you can ring the Royal Mail on their Postcode Enquiry Line (08457 111 222) and they will tell you all you need to know. The correct order for an address is:

ADDRESSEE'S NAME

BUILDING NUMBER OR NAME

STREET NAME (if there is one)

LOCALITY NAME (if there is one)

POST TOWN (in capital letters)

POSTCODE (in capital letters)

There is no need to put commas or full stops at the end of each line and the postcode should always appear on a separate line at the end of the address. It is always a good idea to include a return address on the back of your envelope. If you are writing to Ireland, it is correct to address your envelope 'The Republic of Ireland' or 'Northern Ireland', as appropriate.

EU If you are writing to an EU country (except France and Greece), the street number of the recipient is written after the street name and the postcode is added before the name of the town. If you are writing to France or Greece, however, the street number appears before the street name, as in British addresses, although the postcode still comes before the name of the town.

SAMPLE ENVELOPES:

UK

J. R. Thomas

The Highway Inn

35 Rugby Road

Rugby

RG6 7YT

GERMANY

Herr D. Muller
Sendlinger Str. 34
80331 Munchen
Germany

FRANCE

M. J. LeBlanc
Café 203
235, Rue du Toit
75011 Paris
France

US In order for an envelope to be processed as speedily as possible by the United States postal services, the address should be written entirely in capital letters. The rest of the address should run as follows:

First line: ADDRESSEE'S NAME

Second line: NUMBER, STREET, APARTMENT NUMBER

Third line: CITY, STATE, ZIP CODE

Fourth line: UNITED STATES OF AMERICA

POSTAL ABBREVIATIONS FOR AMERICAN STATES

Alabama	AL	Illinois	IL
Alaska	AK	Indiana	IN
Arizona	AZ	Iowa	IA
Arkansas	AR	Kansas	KS
California	CA	Kentucky	KY
Colorado	CO	Louisiana	LA
Connecticut	CT	Maine	ME
Delaware	DE	Maryland	MD
Florida	FL	Massachusetts	MA
Georgia	GA	Michigan	MI
Hawaii	HI	Minnesota	MN
Idaho	ID	Mississippi	MS
Missouri	MO	Pennsylvania	PA
Montana	MT	Rhode Island	RI
Nebraska	NE	South Carolina	SC
Nevada	NV	South Dakota	SD
New Hampshire	NH	Tennessee	TN
New Jersey	NJ	Texas	TX
New Mexico	NM	Utah	UT
New York	NY	Vermont	VT
North Carolina	NC	Virginia	VA
North Dakota	ND	Washington	WA
Ohio	OH	West Virginia	WV
Oklahoma	OK	Wisconsin	WI
Oregon	OR	Wyoming	WY

SAMPLE ENVELOPE

Ms H. Lovely

341-U E14th ST

CHAPEL POINT

NC 23457

UNITED STATES OF AMERICA

TYPES OF POSTAGE

There is a range of different possibilities open to you when you want to post your letter. You should, naturally, always place the stamp in an obvious place, generally the top right-hand corner of the envelope. Which postal service you choose depends on how soon you want your letter to get to its destination; how important it is to you; how important it is to the recipient; and how valuable the contents are.

If you wish your letter to get to its destination on the next working day, you should always use first-class mail. The earlier in the day that you post your letter, of course, the more likely it is to reach its destination when it is supposed to. If you are sending less urgent items, you may wish to use second-class post, which costs less and means that your letter will arrive within three days.

When choosing how to post your letter, don't just think about yourself. You may think it's a good idea to save a few pennies, but to the recipient this decision may just appear miserly. And the envelope is the first thing the recipient will see.

✔ **DON'T ruin the good impression a well-written letter can make
for the sake of saving a few pence.**

Standard mail is collected from all post boxes and offices six or seven
days a week. If you choose, you can pay under £10 a year to use your
own private letter box as a collection point. If you send your standard
mail without a stamp, or with an insufficient amount of postage, then
it still gets delivered but the recipient has to make up the difference
between what you paid and what you should have paid. This is clearly
an unimpressive business tactic, so it's always worth going to the post
office to have your letters weighed if you think there might be an excess.

If, for some reason, your letter never gets to the prospective recipient,
then eventually it will be sent back to you, but this may take months.

FRANKING

In large offices, it may be easier to control postage systems by the use of
a postage meter or franking machine. Stamps are fiddly little things and
can easily get lost or stuck on to the wrong envelope. A franking
machine may help to avoid these problems and also makes the postage
of vast numbers of envelopes a much simpler enterprise.

A franking machine can be purchased from a number of approved
suppliers. Formerly, in order to use a franking machine, the machine
itself had to be presented at a specified office in order to pre-purchase
a certain amount of postage. Nowadays this operation can be
performed electronically. There are electronic scales attached to the
machine which will display the price of postage automatically.

The date of postage is set automatically at the start of each day. Clearly,
all the envelopes must be placed in the machine in the same direction,
otherwise it won't work. Once you get going, however, it can be an
extremely speedy process, simply threading the envelopes through the
machine and then watching them come out the other end with the
distinctive white paper ribbon in the top right-hand corner on which is
now printed, in red, the date and the cost of the postage.

Franked mail is also of benefit to large businesses because it does not need to be postmarked and is, consequently, sorted more quickly.

SPECIAL DELIVERY

Special delivery is a fast, reliable postage system which, for an additional fee, guarantees next-day delivery for first-class letters. Special delivery aims to:

- Track your item constantly throughout the day so that the Royal Mail can chart its progress.

- Record the time at which it is finally delivered, when someone will sign for it.

- Leave a card for the recipient if there is no one at home to receive it.

- Allow you to confirm delivery by supplying you with a number you can ring for confirmation.

If your letter does not arrive by 12 noon the next day, you are entitled to claim a compensation package which is based on the actual loss suffered, up to a maximum figure, provided you claim within 14 days. Fees for special delivery currently start at around £3.50.

RECORDED DELIVERY

Recorded delivery is a service designed to ensure safe, and confirmed, delivery. The Post Office issues a certificate of postage to the sender and obtains a signature on delivery of the letter. It provides certainty. It is the most widely used service for the delivery of legal documents and certificates which are not, in themselves, valuable but which you need to know have arrived at their destination. The fee for recorded delivery is considerably less than that for special delivery (currently around 65p) but compensation in case of loss is reduced and next-day delivery is not guaranteed.

REGISTERED POST

This is an international service which works in a similar way to inland recorded delivery. Letters are signed for at every stage of their journey and on final delivery to the addressee. It offers a limited compensation package if items get lost, but this is partly dependent on the destination.

An international service called Swiftair is available to and from foreign countries if you want your letter to go with extra speed. Swiftair packages receive extra care.

POSTE RESTANTE

If you are travelling in the UK and constantly moving around, you may find it easier to have all your letters delivered to one particular post office to which you can go for a period of up to three months in order to collect your mail. This service is called 'poste restante', meaning 'remaining at the post office', and you can collect your poste restante simply by showing proof of identity at your selected post office. Clearly, this service is becoming increasingly out of date since most hardened travellers now have email addresses and visit cybercafes to collect their mail. Email communication also means that your information will be right up to date, which is crucial if you are trying to arrange to meet your friend in Jakarta.

PO BOX

A PO Box is handy if you are conducting a limited business campaign and do not want hundreds of replies turning up at your home address. Or if you just want your home address to remain unknown. Mail posted to the box is held inside the post office until you pick it up.

BUSINESS REPLY SERVICE

This is a service which allows businesses to obtain an answer from clients without putting the client to the expense, or hassle, of obtaining a stamp. If you want to use a business reply service, you simply obtain a licence from the local post office which will permit you to enclose reply-paid cards or leaflets in your correspondence with customers. A deposit of around a month's postage is likely to be incurred and the design of your reply card must follow specific regulations. This service is very popular with businesses sending out blind mailshots – it costs the price of postage and the licence plus a little bit extra.

FORWARDING MAIL

If you move house, you can have your mail forwarded to you at a new permanent or temporary address by first-class post in the UK (or even abroad) for a period of up to two years. You simply go to your local post office, fill in a redirection form and pay a fee of around £35 a year. This service is also available to business customers.

If mail is wrongly delivered to you, you should always try to forward it on to the correct address. If you do not know this address, then you simply strike through the address on the envelope and mark it instead with the words 'return to sender'. You do not need to add a new stamp. If the document appears to be a piece of junk mail and is addressed to someone who lived in your house three years ago, it does not really seem worth the effort to forward this on to the prospective recipient. Generally speaking, if the sender's post was in any way important to the recipient, he or she would have informed the sender of the change of address within the last three years. Use your common sense.

SMALL PACKETS

Parcelforce is the parcels division of the Royal Mail and is now the UK's largest express carrier service. It offers a regular service which will guarantee that your parcel is delivered by 9.00 a.m. the next working day; there is also a service called International Datapost which guarantees next-day delivery to over 212 countries. The advantage of using Parcelforce for this service is that you can take your parcel into any post office, or indeed have it collected from your house. Parcelforce also offers a slightly cheaper, slightly less reliable range of services which might guarantee, for example, delivery within two working days to major European cities.

When sending a parcel you should follow basic guidelines and make sure that it does not contain any prohibited items. You should clearly label the package with the following information:

- Recipient's name.

- Recipient's full address, including postcode.

- Recipient's telephone number.

- Sender's name, address and telephone number.

✔ **DO make sure that all relevant documentation is clearly filled out and visible.**

✔ **DO try to ensure that the contents are securely packaged and always obtain a proof of postage at the post office counter as well as a consignment number.**

PRIVATE MAIL SYSTEMS

There are now a number of private mail systems available, all of which may provide the same, or similar, services as the Royal Mail. You can have your own mail box at one of these outlets. If the shop is much closer to you than a regular post office, then it might be handy to use it, but do bear in mind that they may still have to use the facilities of the Royal Mail and that their shop may have fewer collection times than a regular post office. The cost of postage, however, will be identical. Various industries, like the law, have their own internal subscription services for sending documents. The legal system's is called Document Exchange and serves all the major solicitors and chambers – it allows for the safe delivery of specialist documents such as briefs. If you work in a specialist industry, ask your colleagues if such a service exists.

COURIER FIRMS

Courier firms are fast but expensive. 'Biking' your mail can mean that your letter will reach its destination within an hour.

✔ **DO give a courier absolutely specific instructions.**

✔ **DO ensure that there will be someone at the other end.**

✔ **DO reserve couriers for urgent deliveries only.**

CONVENTIONAL ABBREVIATIONS OF UK COUNTY NAMES

(Counties not listed here do not have a standard abbreviation in general use.)

Bedfordshire	**Beds**
Berkshire	**Berks**
Buckinghamshire	**Bucks**
Caerphilly	**Caer**
Cambridgeshire	**Cambs**
East Riding of Yorkshire	**E Yorks**
Gloucestershire	**Glos**
Hampshire	**Hants**
Hertfordshire	**Herts**
Isle of Man	**I o M**
Isle of Wight	**I o W**
Lancashire	**Lancs**
Leicestershire	**Leics**
Lincolnshire	**Lincs**
Middlesex	**Middx**
North East Lincolnshire	**NE Lincs**
North Lincolnshire	**N Lincs**
North Yorkshire	**N Yorks**
Northamptonshire	**Northants**
Northumberland	**Northd**
Nottinghamshire	**Notts**

Oxfordshire	Oxon
South Gloucestershire	S Glos
Staffordshire	Staffs
Shropshire	Salop
Warwickshire	Warks
Wiltshire	Wilts
Worcestershire	Worcs
Yorkshire	Yorks

FORMS OF ADDRESS

ROYALTY

THE QUEEN

Addressing envelope: The Private Secretary to Her Majesty the Queen

Salutation: Dear Sir (or Madam if the Private Secretary is a woman)

THE DUKE OF EDINBURGH

Addressing envelope: The Private Secretary to His Royal Highness the Duke of Edinburgh

Salutation: Dear Sir (or Madam if the Private Secretary is a woman)

ROYAL PRINCES AND PRINCESSES

Addressing envelope: His/Her Royal Highness, The Prince/Princess [first name]

Salutation: Your Royal Highness

ROYAL DUKES AND DUCHESSES

Addressing envelope: His/Her Royal Highness, The Duke/Duchess of [place name]

Salutation: Your Royal Highness

ARISTOCRACY

DUKES AND DUCHESSES

Addressing envelope: The Duke/Duchess of [place name]

Salutation: Dear Duke/Duchess

EARLS AND COUNTESSES

Addressing envelope: The Earl/Countess of [place name]

Salutation: Dear Lord/Lady [place name]

BARONS AND THEIR WIVES

Addressing envelope: The Lord/Lady [place name]

Salutation: Dear Lord/Lady [place name]

HONOURABLES (CHILDREN OF ARISTOCRACY)

Addressing envelope: The Honourable (or The Hon.) [full name]

Salutation: Dear Mr/Miss [surname]

KNIGHTS AND THEIR WIVES

Addressing envelope: Sir/Lady [full name]

Salutation: Dear Sir [first name] or Lady [surname]

DAMES

Addressing envelope: Dame [full name]

Salutation: Dear [full name]

GOVERNMENT MINISTERS

THE PRIME MINISTER

Addressing envelope: The Rt Hon. [full name] MP

Salutation: Dear Prime Minister

THE CHANCELLOR OF THE EXCHEQUER

Addressing envelope: The Rt Hon. [full name] MP

Salutation: Dear Chancellor

SECRETARIES OF STATE

Addressing envelope: The Rt Hon. [full name], PC, MP;
or by appointment only, e.g. The Foreign Secretary

Salutation: Dear Secretary of State or Dear [appointment]

MINISTERS

Addressing envelope: [full name], Esq., MP; or by appointment

Salutation: Dear Minister

MEMBERS OF PARLIAMENT

Addressing envelope: [full name] Esq., MP; or [full name] MP

Salutation: Dear Mr/Mrs/Miss/Ms [surname]

THE CLERGY (CHURCH OF ENGLAND)

ARCHBISHOPS

Addressing envelope: The Most Reverend and Rt Hon, the Lord Archbishop of [place name]

Salutation: Dear Archbishop

BISHOPS

Addressing envelope: The Right Reverend the Lord Bishop of [place name]

Salutation: Dear Bishop

DEANS

Addressing envelope: The Very Reverend the Dean of [place name]

Salutation: Dear Dean or Dear Mrs Dean

ARCHDEACONS

Addressing envelope: The Venerable the Archdeacon of [place name]

Salutation: Dear Archdeacon or Dear Mr Archdeacon

VICARS AND RECTORS

Addressing envelope: The Reverend [full name]

Salutation: Dear Mr [surname]; Dear Father [surname]

(ROMAN CATHOLIC CHURCH)

THE POPE

Addressing envelope: His Holiness the Pope

Salutation: Your Holiness or Most Holy Father

CARDINALS

Addressing envelope: His Eminence the Cardinal Archbishop of [place name]; or (if not an archbishop) His Eminence Cardinal [surname]

Salutation: Dear Cardinal [surname]; or Cardinal [surname]

ARCHBISHOPS

Addressing envelope: His Grace the Archbishop of [place name]

Salutation: Dear Archbishop [surname]; or Your Grace

BISHOPS

Addressing envelope: The right Reverend [full name], Bishop of [place name]

Salutation: My Lord Bishop or Dear Bishop [surname]

MONSIGNORS

Addressing envelope: The Reverend Monsignor [full name] or The Reverend Monsignor

Salutation: Dear Monsignor [surname]

(CHURCH OF SCOTLAND)

MINISTERS

Addressing envelope: The Reverend [full name]

Salutation: Dear Mr/Mrs [surname] or Dear Minister

(JEWISH)

THE CHIEF RABBI

Addressing envelope: The Chief Rabbi Dr [full name]

Salutation: Dear Chief Rabbi

RABBIS

Addressing envelope: Rabbi [full name]

Salutation: Dear Rabbi [surname] or Dr if applicable

LEGAL DIGNITARIES

THE LORD CHANCELLOR

Addressing envelope: The Rt Hon, [full peerage title], the Lord Chancellor

Salutation: Dear Lord Chancellor or My Lord

THE LORD CHIEF JUSTICE

Addressing envelope: The Rt Hon, The Lord Chief Justice of England, PC

Salutation: Dear Lord Chief Justice or My Lord

LORD JUSTICE-GENERAL (OF SCOTLAND)

Addressing envelope: The Rt Hon, The Lord Justice-General, PC

Salutation: Dear Justice-General or My Lord

MASTER OF THE ROLLS

Addressing envelope: The Master of the Rolls

Salutation: Dear Master of the Rolls

HIGH COURT JUDGES

Addressing envelope: The Hon. Mr/Mrs Justice [surname]

Salutation: Dear Judge/Madam

CIRCUIT COURT JUDGES

Addressing envelope: His/Her Honour Judge [surname]

Salutation: (Dear) Sir/Madam

QUEEN'S COUNSEL

Addressing envelope: [full name], Esq. QC/Mrs [surname], QC

Salutation: Dear Mr/Mrs [surname]

LOCAL GOVERNMENT/CIVIC OFFICIALS

LORD OR LADY MAYORESS

Addressing envelope: The Right Worshipful the Lord Mayor of [place name]/the Lady Mayoress of [place name]: except for London, York, Belfast and Cardiff, which is The Rt. Hon. the Lord Mayor of [place name]

Salutation: Mr Lord Mayor (formal), Dear Lord Mayor (social); My Lady Mayoress (formal), Dear Lady Mayoress (social)

MAYORS AND MAYORESSES

Addressing envelope: The Right Worshipful the Mayor/Mayoress of [place name]

Salutation: Sir/Madam

COUNCILLORS

Addressing envelope: Councillor Mr/Mrs/rank [full name]

Salutation: Dear Councillor

ORDINARY PEOPLE

MARRIED WOMEN

Addressing envelope: Mrs [first and surname]

Salutation: Dear Mrs [married surname]

DAUGHTERS

Addressing envelope: Miss [first and surname]; the eldest daughter may be just Miss [surname]

Salutation: Dear Miss [surname]

WIDOWS

Addressing envelope: Mrs [husband's first and surname]

Salutation: Dear Mrs [married surname]

DIVORCEES

Addressing envelope: Mrs [own first name, married surname]

Salutation: Dear Mrs [married surname]